ADVANCE PRAISE

"*The Project Revolution* is a breakthrough in the way we look at and understand projects. The concepts Antonio presents are so insightful yet simple, that they will become part of everyone's day-to-day toolkit. This book will help leaders and organizations excel at the increasing amount of projects they have to carry out to succeed in today's fast-changing world."

MARSHALL GOLDSMITH

Thinkers50 #1 Executive Coach and *New York Times* #1 bestselling author of *Triggers, Mojo* and *What Got You Here Won't Get You There*

"Projects today are the key unit of work. Understanding projects, leading projects, teaming across expertise boundaries in new and shifting configurations, and relishing the novelty of new challenges have thus become the competencies that people must develop to thrive in the modern economy. Nieto-Rodriguez shows us how."

AMY C. EDMONDSON

Novartis Professor of Leadership and Management,
Harvard Business School and author of *The Fearless Organization*

"In our ever-changing world – amidst a growing freelance economy – projects have become the new way of delivering work and creating value. *The Project Revolution* provides a proven method for both current and aspiring entrepreneurs to succeed in this new reality."

DORIE CLARK

Adjunct Professor, Duke University Fuqua School of Business
and bestselling author of *Stand Out* and *Entrepreneurial You*

AUG - - 2019

"This book leaves no doubt that the Project Revolution has started and that it is disruptive. Projects are part of everything we do; big, small, professional, personal, local and worldwide, they change the world we live in now and in the future. Their impact is a world-changing revolution. Antonio identifies five main implications of the massive disruption of the project revolution form Careers to Democracy and how they will be reshaped by the revolution. You will want to know how these disruptions are going to change your world and how you can prepare to deal with them."

JAMES R. SNYDER
Founder of the Project Management Institute,
First President and Past Chair of the Board,
worked most of his career at GlaxoSmithKline

"Read the book and you will be persuaded that if projects are not the most powerful driver of business, achievement and entire economies today, they soon will be – and should be. Nieto-Rodriquez provides the Project Canvas as a fast-moving, intuitive tool to improve efficiency, elevate project managers to true organizational leaders and change makers and to ensure that projects align with core strategic objectives and add value. Good project management facilitated by this book can be conscious and constant, rather than happily accidental – or not, as the case may be. Projects can be the disruptive catalyst to changing business rather than just running it; projects can change the world."

WHITNEY JOHNSON
Thinkers50 Leading Management Thinkers,
bestselling author of *Build an A Team*

"Antonio Nieto-Rodriguez's book is an eye opener in a highly disruptive environment with the strong need to stay focused at the same time. Project management is in the need to assign diversity and flexible methodologies to a rocketing amount of business critical topics. This book is instrumental to understand the need and to find pragmatic solutions for this ambiguous challenge."

ANDREAS JOEHLE
CEO, Hartmann Group

"A brilliant piece of work! Antonio turns project management into this refreshing and thought-provoking book that will resonate with every entrepreneur and women like me that want to succeed in the business world. Thanks to the simplicity of the Project Canvas, I have been able to introduce corporate napping and its benefits in many companies. *The Project Revolution* will certainly be my go-to-guide for many years to come."

CLARISSE HALAWANI
CEO and Founder, CorpNap

"Purpose driven, passionate people guided by their values create amazing outcomes – Antonio Nieto-Rodriguez has beautifully laid out how process linked to purpose will help you lead people through the fast pace of today to amazing outcomes."

GARRY RIDGE
President and CEO, WD-40 Company

"Antonio's new book is the catalyst and essential read for project managers around the world. As strategy shifts in many industries to being more experiment centric, projects are going to become more and more critical for achieving excellence in execution. As a result, project managers need a new approach and mind-set. *The Project Revolution* shows you the way and more importantly the how."

ROBIN SPECULAND
Pioneer in Strategy Implementation and bestselling
author of *Excellence in Execution*

"In these rapidly changing times PROJECTS will dominate the modus operandi of successful companies, of successful public sector bodies, of successful civil society organizations, even of successful individuals. Who could better set out than Antonio Nieto-Rodriguez what the project revolution will bring and mean. A must-read for all wanting to shape a better future for others and themselves."

WALTER DEFFAA
Former Director General for Regional and
Urban Policy in the European Commission

"Projects touch every part of our lives. Antonio has a knack for analyzing and extracting the key messages from what may appear on the surface to be daunting issues. In an equally entertaining and pragmatic style, he has distilled his analysis, research and many years of experience into invaluable teachings and take-aways which are within every reader's reach."

LINDSEY DOMINGO
Trustee, Bridges to Prosperity and former Partner
with Ernst Young and PricewaterhouseCoopers

"Whether you work in a multinational organization or a smaller business, the way we work is changing. As Antonio Nieto-Rodriguez so effectively illustrates, projects are the backbone of how work gets done and a well-run project is the differentiator between success or failure, or even worse, interminable inertia. While projects by their nature are temporary, the value of Antonio's ideas and frameworks will have permanent value. I'm ready to join the Project Revolution!"

LAINE JOELSON COHEN
Director of Leadership and Executive Development, Citi
and executive coach

"Those living in the midst of a revolution are often blissfully unaware that it is happening. Thankfully, Antonio Nieto-Rodriguez has distilled his considerable expertise and experience into a compelling manifesto on the coming Project Revolution. Projects are on the march and those who can turn ideas into reality by leading people through project-based work will play a critical role in shaping the future of society, government and industry. Ignore this book at your own peril!"

DR TONY O'DRISCOLL
Academic Director, Adaptive Strategic Execution Program,
Duke University's Fuqua School of Business

"Antonio Nieto-Rodriguez is ahead of the curve and he's catching us up in *The Project Revolution*. All of the work I do is already project-based, and if that's not the case for you, it soon will be. This is an indispensable guide for what to do – and how to do it – when that happens. Eminently readable, profoundly inspirational, and exceptionally practical, *The Project Revolution* is a must-read for anyone who works."

PETER BREGMAN
CEO, Bregman Partners and bestselling author of
18 Minutes, Four Seconds and *Leading With Emotional Courage*

"A captivating, worldwide view and statistically supported collection and reflection of insights into the world of project management. This book explores how project intelligence is enabling modern leaders to innovate, adapt and achieve results faster."

TODD HUTCHISON

Global Chairman, International Institute
of Legal Project Management

"*The Project Revolution* is an easy read about the fundamental skills necessary in project management. Antonio Nieto-Rodriguez has gathered an impressive amount of stories and data to support his view that all business leaders are, to a certain extent, project managers. This claim is, of course, correct."

INGMAR HÖHMANN

Senior Editor, Harvard Business Manager

"Antonio lives, breathes, sees and, most importantly, elucidates management through the prism of projects. His project narratives are captivating, a product of intense experiences throughout his professional life. Make no mistake: Antonio brings a project revolution, and he does so with a smile and the necessary self-deprecation."

MANUEL HENSMANS

Professor of Strategy at the Solvay Brussels School of
Economics and Management, ULB and author of bestseller
Strategic Transformation: Changing While Winning

"*The Project Revolution* contains the absolute best practices in the project management space that are easily applicable to any project management initiative or program – and are right in line with the practices we support at Best Practice Institute – whether it is organizational change, talent management, or an operational/strategic change, the practices, principles and real-world pragmatism in the book are right in line with the fast pace of change required for more agile, rapid cycle deployment balanced with extreme precision and excellence in practice."

LOUIS CARTER

CEO and Founder, Best Practice Institute
and author of *In Great Company*

"What I like most about this book is that Antonio looks at project management from a broad perspective. Once you realize that many things in life are projects, the need for solid project management skills becomes even more clear. Working with Antonio over the past years has made it clear for me that the basic skills for managing projects are all-round and that you can benefit from them in every aspect of your professional – and even private life."

ASTRID DE WAEL

Senior Account Manager Executive Education,
Vlerick Business School

"Project management is the unsung hero of the skillset of the future. Antonio Nieto-Rogriguez's *The Project Revolution* – with its global mindset, rigorous data and captivating style – brings to light the need for all of us to think in projects. The insights here are essential for all leaders and professionals who want to innovate and keep up with the future. And have you ever read a book about project management that you just couldn't put down? Welcome to the Project Revolution."

ALISA COHEN

Executive coach and thoughtleader, named one of
INC's Top 100 Leadership Speakers for 2018

"In these times of incredible change, *The Project Revolution* replaces traditional roadmaps with a project-based approach to life, work and organizations. A must read for everyone who is driven by bringing ideas to life."

AYSE BIRSEL
Author of *Design the Life You Love* and
one of Fast Company's Most Creative People

"Antonio clearly articulates how and why work is gravitating toward projects. More importantly, his frameworks and stories ensure that people feel prepared – and excited – about starting and leading projects successfully."

DEEPA PRAHALAD
Business strategist and thoughtleader,
co-author of *Predictable Magic: Unleash the Power of Design Strategy to Transform Your Business*

"With ever-shortening business cycles and the concept of 'business as usual' barely existing, projects have become even more important to organizations. Through this book, project managers can benefit from Antonio's world-wide experience and pick up his genuine passion for project management!"

STEPHEN SMALLBONE
Head of Portfolio Management, Euronext

"Antonio brings to life the topic of project management, often seen as too technical or just overlooked by business leaders. The reader discovers that good project management is critical to address real problems and challenges whose solution is not often thought of as a project. A refreshing book on a classic topic."

FABRIZIO SALVADOR

Professor of Operations and Technology and Director of Applied Research, Instituto de Empresa (IE) Business School

"That we live exponential times is evident. What isn't as evident is the impact that the convergence of exponential technologies is going to have. It will change the way corporations will need to react in order to survive and I believe that, like Roger Martin says, corporations will have to change towards project management cultures, abhorring from existing paradigms. Antonio lands these ideas in a book we all should contemplate as a necessary tool."

FEDERICO FERNÁNDEZ DE SANTOS ORTI

Senior Editor, *Executive Excellence*

"You need read no further than Chapter 1 to realize Antonio provides headlights to a future of global transformations that affect the way leaders strategically plan projects and execute them with agility. I cherish Antonio's ability to synthesize actual project histories with quantitative trend analysis that has given me a better understanding of the future of projects."

STEVE DELGROSSO

Former Director of Project Management Center of Excellence at IBM Global Business Services, 2014 PMI Chair, PMO Evangelist

"*The Project Revolution* is a must read for leaders at all levels to get both a macro and micro conceptual understanding of how projects are impacting organizations as a silent disruptor. Most important, Antonio provides a roadmap on how to navigate a successful project and the common pitfalls to avoid. The book is wonderfully practical and thought-provoking. Antonio has done it again!"

TAAVO GODTFREDSEN
Vice President and Executive Producer
for Leadership Solutions, Skillsoft
and Creator of Five@5:00

"In his book, Antonio observes: 'The emergence of projects as the economic engine of our times is silent but incredibly disruptive and powerful.' Whether or not you like to believe this is irrelevant. The reality is that through his personal experiences, both good and bad, and his dedicated study of all kinds of projects around the world, Antonio is able foresee the future. In fact, this is not just of projects and programs, but the whole set up of effective and beneficial governance of the world through projects. If you want to be with it, read Antonio's latest book for practical guidance."

MAX WIDEMAN
Founder of Project Management Wisdom,
Founder of The Wideman Education Foundation (Canada)
and primary author of PMI's® first PMBOK document

"From the time I first met him Antonio has held an absolute conviction that the success of humanity lay in how well we organize around projects. Since then he has been an advocate for project management within the corridors of organizations and governments, a journey that has gained him recognition as one of the foremost management thinkers of our time. In *The Project Revolution*, Antonio prepares us to lead and play a critical role in this project-driven world."

YOHAN ABRAHAMS
Portfolio Manager, Highways Infrastructure Transport of
London and Past President, PMI UK Chapter

Published by
LID Publishing Limited
The Record Hall, Studio 204,
16-16a Baldwins Gardens,
London EC1N 7RJ, UK

524 Broadway, 11th Floor, Suite 08-120,
New York, NY 10012, US

info@lidpublishing.com
www.lidpublishing.com

www.businesspublishersroundtable.com

Printed in Great Britain by TJ International
ISBN: 978-1-911498-99-5

Cover design: Caroline Li
Page design: Matthew Renaudin

THE PROJECT REVOLUTION

ANTONIO NIETO-RODRIGUEZ

HOW TO SUCCEED IN A PROJECT DRIVEN WORLD

LONDON   NEW YORK   SHANGHAI
MADRID   BARCELONA   BOGOTA
MEXICO CITY   MONTERREY   BUENOS AIRES

CONTENTS

ACKNOWLEDGMENTS

Writing a book is a highly complex project. It provides great satisfaction when you receive the first printed copy, but it is a marathon constantly on your mind for months and sometimes years. The pressure escalates when the deadline approaches at fast speed and you still have many pages to write. It's even more challenging when the end date is in the middle of the summer, just after a FIFA World Cup.

It is impossible to accomplish such an endeavour without the support of family. Thanks to my exceptional wife – Clarisse, my amazing children – Laura, Alexander, Selma and Lucas, my caring parents – Maria Jose and Juan Antonio, and my brilliant brothers – Javi, Iñaki and Jose Miguel.

I would like to thank Stuart and Des for their advice, as well as the LID publishing team for their trust in my work. And to all the amazing people that contributed by sharing their stories and those who have endorsed my book: it is a privilege to have such world-class experts acknowledging *The Project Revolution*.

Lastly, I want to also dedicate this book to the millions of project managers that with their hard work – often unrecognized – contribute to making a better world.

PLANET PROJECT

**FROM OUR PERSONAL
TO OUR PROFESSIONAL
LIVES, CORPORATIONS TO
GOVERNMENTS, INDIVIDUALS
TO NATIONS, PROJECTS ARE
THE NEW REALITY. WELCOME
TO THE PROJECT REVOLUTION!**

THURSDAY 5 AUGUST 2010, 2PM, ATACAMA DESERT, CHILE[1]

A huge explosion and then the ground shakes, an intense tremble. Deep underground, the San Jose mine has collapsed. It is a terrible disaster but no real surprise. Previous geological instability at the old mine has contributed to a series of lethal accidents in the dozen years leading up to this disaster. A huge rock has fallen and blocked the entry to the mine. A group of miners nearer the entrance manage to escape, but a second group of 33 men remain trapped deep inside, 700 metres underground and five kilometres from the mine's entrance. Emergency officials are unable to communicate with the trapped miners.

Twenty minutes later, the Chilean mining minister, Laurence Golborne, makes a call to the country's president, Sebastián Piñera, who is on an official trip to Colombia, and informs him of the tragic accident. The disaster comes soon after sharp criticism of the government's handling of the Chilean earthquake and tsunami in February 2010, which killed more than 500 Chileans. President Piñera decides to cut short his trip and returns to Chile immediately to visit the mine. On 7 August 2010, after two days of unceasing work by 130 rescuers, President Piñera arrives in the regional capital, Copiapó, 45 kilometres south of the mine in northern Chile. He meets with officials to assess the situation and to hear about the latest setback: another rock fall has blocked the only path that can be used to look for the miners. After two days of searching, it is unclear whether the 33 miners are still alive. The president is informed that the chances of finding the miners is minimal. Unfortunately, mining accidents tend to be fatal.

President Piñera knows that he needs to make a vital decision, a decision that might cost him his tenure. Should he launch a project to find the miners? The chances of finding them are small, very small, and the chances of finding them alive are much smaller still. A rescue mission would also be highly dangerous for all those involved. More lives could be lost. Does he simply accept that there is no chance of success and hope that the Chilean citizens rapidly forget the tragedy? Another one!

SATURDAY 7 AUGUST 2010, 3PM, PERTH, AUSTRALIA

At the same time that President Piñera is wrestling with his major potentially career-changing decision, on the other side of the world on a sunny afternoon in a small church facing the ocean, Mary Smith and Matt Jones say "Yes, I do" to each other, becoming husband and wife. Mary's mother is in tears, happy to see her daughter beautifully dressed in white and having achieved one of her dreams. The rest of the couple's family and friends celebrate the moment with a two-minute round of applause. From the church, the wedding party will head off to Saint Jacques, an exclusive restaurant near the bay of Perth.

Mary and Matt set the date of their wedding, 7 August 2010, precisely 18 months after Matt proposed. As all their friends will tell you, neither Matt nor Mary is good at long-term planning. It is simply not their thing. They are always late when there is a deadline and never plan anything in advance. Most of their decisions are taken ad hoc, often with last-minute changes. Yet, by some kind of magic, on this occasion, the deadline is met with scientific precision and the wedding is an absolute success.

Once the happy decision had been made, Mary and Matt looked for the most appropriate date. They decided to take it easy, not to put too much pressure on themselves. August 2010, about 18 months, seemed to be more than enough time to prepare for the kind of wedding they wanted – something special but not over the top. Looking for a location was easy, as Mary had already thought about that: she wanted to get married where her parents had. After selecting the restaurant – Matt's favourite – they looked at when it was available and decided to get married on the seventh of the month. Next, over a cup of coffee, they considered the activities needed for a successful wedding. They split the work and decided who was responsible for each of the tasks, adding an estimated date of completion. Working backwards, starting with the D-Day they had in mind and plugging in all the various essential activities, they had their first ever project plan. (Their friends suggest it might also be their last!)

Naturally, Mary and Matt were excited about their project. It was a big decision, but it was their big decision, their choice. They talked about progress on their wedding plans every day, taking decisions and adjusting the activities in the plan when needed. They also sought advice from Matt's sister and Mary's close friend, both of whom had recently married. The pressure increased as they approached the big day, to the point that they were having nightmares about being late for the wedding. They had never felt pressure like this ever before, but they found that it helped them focus in completing the missing tasks. The project was a tremendous success. Without them really knowing how, everything went according to plan. The wedding was intimate and memorable, and everybody enjoyed the ceremony and the exquisite feast, and danced until 4am. The Joneses will never forget a truly wonderful day.

SATURDAY 7 AUGUST 2010, 8AM, BERLIN, GERMANY

At a construction site in Schönefeld, 18 kilometres south of the city centre, three people gather to assess the timelines and costs of the new Berlin airport. After four years of construction, the expenses are double the original estimates. Costs have been underestimated, significant scope changes have been introduced and construction flaws have been identified, all of which have had an impact on the quality and timeline of the project. The target opening date of 30 October 2011 is looking terribly unrealistic. Jörg Marks, the head of Project BER, removes his hard hat and sits down to pore over the timings once again with two of his colleagues, all of them working on a Saturday morning once again.

The vision for the new airport was – and still is – persuasive. One of the main goals was for Berlin Brandenburg Airport to become the busiest in Germany, with a projected 45 million passengers annually. It was intended to replace both Berlin Schönefeld Airport and Berlin Tegel Airport and become the single commercial airport serving Berlin and the surrounding state of Brandenburg.

The plans were thorough. The airport's feasibility and preplanning phase took about 15 years. Construction started in 2006, and it was anticipated that the airport would take five years to be built. But, during construction, it gradually became clear that the airport would be significantly more expensive than planned due to poor estimates and important changes in the design. An example of a change from the original scope that had a significant impact on the cost and the schedule was when, with construction under way, one of the key stakeholders, Rainer Schwarz, general manager of the airport management company, seizing on increasing forecasts for air traffic, asked the architect to add north and south 'piers' to the main terminal, turning it from a rectangle into a 'U' and dramatically enlarging the floor space.[2] At a later stage, Schwarz, with the vision of making the airport into a luxury mall, asked to insert into the original plan a second level with shops, boutiques and food courts.

As Marks sits down with his colleagues in August 2010, there is pressure not to delay the opening date from Schwarz and the city's mayor, Klaus Wowereit, who is the project sponsor and chairman of the supervisory board. They don't want to admit that there are problems. Marks decides to inform the public about the issues and to propose a new opening date: 3 June 2012.

The next day, in a hall packed with government officials and journalists, Schwarz sits grimly behind a table with four others, including Mayor Wowereit, and announces the unthinkable: the airport won't open as scheduled.

It is merely a prelude to a debacle that is still unfolding as I write. Today, in late 2018, seven years after the original planned launch day (30 October 2011), the new Berlin Brandenburg International Willy Brandt Airport,[3] billed at one point as Europe's "most modern airport", has yet to open. The latest promise is that it will open in 2020 with total projected costs of €7.9 billion, almost 50% above the approved budget of €5.4 billion. The project has become a €7.9 billion embarrassment and has joined two other notorious project failures – Stuttgart 21, a railway station that was €2 billion over budget, and an €865 million concert hall in Hamburg – in ruining Germany's reputation for order, efficiency and engineering mastery.

SATURDAY 7 AUGUST 2010, 3PM, ATACAMA DESERT, CHILE

Meanwhile, back in Copiapó, Chile, after a couple of hours listening to the rescue team, and understanding that finding the miners alive will be a daunting task, President Piñera goes for a walk around the San Jose mine. He is about to make a decision that will have dramatic consequences. He talks to his press secretary and asks him to call a press conference in the next hour. The crew sets up the paraphernalia required for high-tech communication from one of the most isolated places in South America and the media gathers around. Knowing the entire nation will be watching, President Piñera says that he and the government of Chile are determined to rescue the 33 miners, and that they will put at the disposal of the rescue teams all the means and resources needed to bring the miners back to the surface alive. Although he has strong doubts, he believes that one of the roles of a president is to save human lives.

The day after, Piñera calls the best mining engineer in Chile, Andre Sougarret, and convinces him to lead the rescue efforts. A team of 700 workers are sent to the San Jose mine. They settle down in a base camp, named 'Esperanza', the 'Hope camp'. In an unprecedented move, the mining minister, Laurence Golborne, resides full time in the camp to lead the efforts and act on behalf of the president. The families of the miners are, by now, desperate to receive news about their loved ones. The first attempts to find the miners fail. Golborne promises full transparency in communicating the status of the rescue efforts. The families are updated every two hours.

Despite the setbacks, spirits are high among the rescuers and mine workers. Everyone is working hard towards achieving a common objective.

Traditional mining exploration techniques would take 12 months to find the miners, so this approach is not an option. In an example of how the entire country is helping in the rescue efforts, the national petrochemical company ENAP (Empresa Nacional del Petróleo) offers its advanced sonar technologies, used to identify petrol wells, to help locate the miners.

During the following 17 days, the media and a selection of experts criticize the work, the search locations and the techniques used.

There is mounting pressure from relatives who want to enter the mine. If things go wrong, the cost will be tremendous from the political and judicial points of view.

But on Sunday 22 August, at 5am, Golborne is woken by the lead engineer, who informs him that they have broken into a refuge area in the mine. They are not sure whether the miners are alive, but they believe they have found where they are. When the digging equipment comes out of the ground, in one of the air ducts they see a note, which reads, "We're fine, at shelter, the 33".

In the first few minutes of Wednesday 13 October 2010, 70 days after the accident, the first miner, Florencio Ávalos, is lifted to the surface from 700 metres below the earth in the capsule Fenix, developed with the help of NASA. At a rate of about one per hour, all 33 men are rescued, safe and alive, as President Piñera, Minister Golborne and all the families look on.

To date this is the largest and most successful rescue in the history of mining. It also received a record amount of media coverage, with around a billion viewers (only surpassed by the funeral of Michael Jackson in 2009).

The unbelievable rescue of the Chilean miners, Mary and Matt's memorable wedding and the disastrous, yet-to-be-seen Berlin airport are examples of three projects that happened simultaneously. They are very different projects, with different outcomes – two extremely positive, one an absolute ongoing nightmare.

They are proof of the personal and organizational power of projects. Projects can save lives. Projects can improve lives. Projects can change the landscape of the world.

THE SILENT DISRUPTION

In my quest to learn more about what really makes projects tick – and the reverse – I have come across some incredible achievements.

In Rwanda, for example, after one of the worst genocides in recent human history, an audacious leader, President Paul Kagame, decided to change the country's destiny through Rwanda's Reconstruction and Reconciliation Programme. Twenty years later, 92% of Rwandans feel reconciled.[4] And the country, devastated at that time, has become one of the most advanced in Africa, with one of the world's highest rates of women in parliament (56%).

Or consider the rise of Singapore. In 1961, it was a ruined former British trading colony; today, it is one of the most competitive economies in the world. Prime Minster Lee Kuan Yew's[5] vision was to build an economically sound country that would be robust enough for future generations. The project included establishing the rule of law, efficient government structures, a continuous fight against corruption and overall stability. A cornerstone of the programme was its uncompromising standards for a universally accessible, top-flight public education system – which astutely identified human capital as Singapore's key competitive advantage – supplemented with rigorous application of meritocracy. Singapore is considered one of the most carefully planned cities in the world.

Or think of Dubai, transformed from a fishing town in the middle of the desert to a vibrant and modern city. Or the small Danish city of Odense, which, through an ambitious project transformed itself into one of the most innovative robotics hubs in Europe. Or Curitiba, Brazil's green capital and one of the most environmentally friendly and sustainable cities in Latin America.

Think of the introduction of the euro in 2002, or of when the Swedish decided to switch traffic to the other side of the road during the night of 3 September 1967.

Some of the most fascinating technological achievements have been, in essence, brilliant projects: John F. Kennedy's vision to send the first man to the moon by the end of the 1960s; the creation of the Boeing 777, a technological masterpiece in the aircraft industry; and Project Purple in 2006, which built the first smartphone, the iPhone, and transformed the entire telecommunications industry.

Last but not least, there are hundreds of amazing personal projects – achievements reached under extremely adverse conditions or simply personal dreams that are made reality through a project.

All this is nothing new. Projects are timeless and universal. The construction of the pyramids in Egypt, the development of modern cities, the Marshall Plan, the Apollo space programme, the creation of the European Union – all these achievements were the result of ideas being turned into reality through projects. Project-based work is the engine that generates the major accomplishments of our civilization; it has stimulated society to advance and often go beyond long-established scientific and cultural limits.

Projects change the world. Projects make impossible dreams possible.

The behavioural and social sciences endorse the idea that there are a few ways of working and collaborating that are particularly motivating and inspiring for people working on a project. These are that a project should have ambitious goals, a higher purpose and a clear deadline. You have probably noticed that what people tend to remember most clearly from their entire careers is the projects they work on – often the successful ones, but also the failed ones.

According to recent research, the number of individuals working in project-based roles will increase from 66 million (in 2017) to 88 million (forecast 2027). And the value of economic activity worldwide that is project oriented will grow from $12 trillion (in 2013) to $20 trillion (forecast 2027).[6] Those are millions of projects requiring millions of project managers per year.

Projects are on the march. FIGURE I (on the next page) is illustrative of this massive, yet unnoticed, disruption. Based on research using Google Ngram Viewer,[7] the graph shows the number of times the world 'project' appears across a vast corpus of printed sources published between 1900 and 2000 compared with other common management and business terms, such as 'strategy', 'operations', 'sales', 'leadership', 'innovation' and 'talent'. This is what I describe as the Project Revolution.

This silent disruption is impacting not only organizations but also the very nature of work, and our entire professional lives. The traditional one-company career path of previous generations is now a distant memory. Today, people happily and fruitfully change jobs and employers a number of times during their careers. I believe that this trend will accelerate and that professional careers will become a sequence of projects. Another notable trend related to this is the growth in self-employment – according to Quartz at Work, an HR consulting company, the number of Americans working for themselves could triple by 2020.[8] They will be, effectively, managing a portfolio of projects.

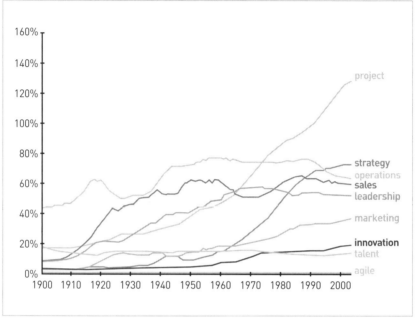

According to Google's Ngram viewer, 'Project' is the most popular of this set of words frequently used in business and management, and its popularity is only increasing

A GLOBAL REVOLUTION

The more you look, the more projects you will see. On my desk, I have a bushel of examples.

For example, in December 2016, the US Senate unanimously approved the Program Management Improvement and Accountability Act (PMIAA),[9] which will enhance accountability and best practices in project and programme management throughout the US federal government. The PMIAA will reform federal programme management policy in four important ways:

- creating a formal job series and career path for programme and project managers in the federal government
- developing a standards-based programme and project management policy across the federal government
- recognizing the essential role of executive sponsorship and engagement by designating a senior executive in federal agencies to be responsible for programme and project management policy and strategy
- sharing knowledge of successful approaches to programme and project management through an interagency council on programme and project management.

In the UK, on 6 January 2017, the Association for Project Management was awarded a Royal Charter.[10] The receipt of a Royal Charter marks a significant achievement in the evolution of project management and will have positive implications for those who make, and seek to make, a career in this field. The Charter recognizes the project management profession, rewards the association that champions its cause and provides opportunities for those who practice its disciplines.

I also have a note from a conference I attended where a senior IBM talent executive said, "Soon in IBM, we will no longer have job descriptions, we will have only project descriptions." Sounds like progress!

He is not alone. The Richards Group is the largest independently owned ad agency in the US, with billings of $1.28 billion, revenue of $170 million and more than 650 employees. Stan Richards, its founder and CEO, removed almost all of its management layers and job titles, leaving only that of project manager.[11]

In another example, in 2016, Nike was looking to fill a vacancy at its European headquarters. The job description was Corporate Strategy & Development Manager for the European, Middle East & Africa (EMEA) Region. Such a job would traditionally entail strategic planning, market analysis and competitive intelligence competencies. To my surprise, instead the job was described as 'project management'. This meant that Nike was looking for someone who could implement transversal and strategic projects for its strategy function. This was a clear shift of focus and culture: from planning and day-to-day activities to implementation and projects. And Nike is not alone – I have seen similar job descriptions for strategy functions at UPS, Amazon and others.

WE ARE ALL
REVOLUTIONARIES NOW

The emergence of projects as the economic engine of our times is silent but incredibly disruptive and powerful.

And this massive disruption is not only impacting the way organizations are managed. Every aspect of our lives is becoming a set of projects. The main implications, which I will cover in this book, are as follows:

- **Education**: For centuries, learning was achieved by memorizing hefty books and mountains of written material. Today, the leading educational systems, starting from early ages, apply the concept of teaching projects. Applying theories and experimenting through projects has proven to be a much better learning method, and soon it will become the norm. **What are the implications of this for how we are taught and the organizations that provide education?**
- **Careers**: Not so long ago, professional careers were made in only one organization. Throughout the 20th century, most people worked for a single company. Today we are likely to work for several companies, and at some point we will most probably become self-employed, working primarily on projects. This sort of career is best approached as a set of projects in which we apply the lessons we have learned from previous jobs, companies and industries while developing ourselves for our next career move, often not known in advance. **What does the project career mean for employers and employees?**
- **Corporate governance**: Boards play a critical role in value creation and long-term organizational success. In the current turbulent times, providing direction and prioritizing initiatives have become essential competencies for boards. When organizations execute too many strategic projects without clear prioritization from the top, they will be spread too thinly: teams will fight

for resources, commitments to contribute to certain projects will not be respected, and most projects will fail to meet their initial cost, time and benefit estimates. Conversely, ignorance of the accountability duties by directors in these matters is a weakness in corporate governance that can have devastating consequences for corporations, destroying a vast amount of value and often bringing corporations to the verge of collapse. **How will our organizations be restructured and governed to maximize the value creation and impact of projects?**

- **Democracy**: The current crisis that we are seeing in political systems around the world has led academics and others to propose new ways of governing countries. One of the most revolutionary experiments was carried out in Ireland. The Convention on the Constitution, established by the Irish government in 2012, addressed a number of potential constitutional reforms, including whether to change the electoral system or to reform the parliament. The novelty was that each topic was being tackled through a project. One third of the convention's membership consisted of members of the Irish parliament, and two thirds was made up of ordinary citizens who were selected at random from the Irish population and worked on the project in a limited time frame. **How will democracy be reshaped and revitalized by projects?**

- **Economic theory and prosperity indicators**: Progress has traditionally been measured based on purchasing power or per capita income. But what really marks progress is something else in the background: throughout history, both societies and individuals have gained a greater capacity to carry out projects. Traditional indicators, stemming from economic theory, were fine when the world was more predictable, but that is no longer the case. In the near future, we might be looking at economic indicators based on the real capacity of a country, or company, to carry out its projects. That could be a more suitable indicator of economic and social power. **What kinds of new project-related indicators should economists introduce to measure effective progress and prosperity?**

My prediction is that by 2025, regardless of the industry or sector, senior leaders and managers will spend at least 60% of their time selecting, prioritizing and driving the execution of projects. We will all become project leaders – despite never having been trained to be so!

In this new landscape, projects are becoming the essential model to deliver change and create value. In Germany, for example, approximately 40% of the turnover and the activities of German companies are performed as projects. This is only going to increase.[12] In fact, similar percentages can be found in most Western economies. The figures are even higher in China and some of the other leading Asian economies,[13] where project-based work has been an essential element in their economic emergence. The so-called gig economy is driven by projects. Make no mistake, we are witnessing the rise of the project economy.

And the good news is that project-based work is human-centric. My belief is that project-based work will increase the focus on people. Projects cannot be carried out by machines; they need humans to do the work. Humans must gather together around the purpose of the project, dividing up the work, bonding, interacting and addressing emotional aspects to create a high-performing team. Technology will of course play a role in projects. It will improve the selection of projects and increase the chances of success. But technology will be an enabler and not the goal. The Project Revolution will be led by people, not robots. It will be led by people like you.

THE PROJECT CANVAS

One of the main purposes of this book is to provide you with an easy-to-apply framework to help you succeed in this new project-driven world. After studying hundreds of successful and failed projects ranging from small individual ones (such as refurbishing a house) to the transformation of Rwanda after the 1994 genocide, I have developed a simple tool – the Project Canvas – that can be applied by any individual, team, organization or country.

The framework, which covers the basic principles and funda-mentals of projects that everyone should know, is practical and easy to implement. It is a proven tool that will assist you in leading projects more successfully and in making your dreams a reality.

The Project Canvas is composed of four major domains that are broken down into 14 dimensions:

- **Why**: the **rationale** and **expected benefits**, as well as the **purpose and passion** for launching and implementing the project successfully
- **Who**: the **accountability** and the **governance** that will ensure the project is resourced and delivered
- **What**, **How** and **When**: the **hard aspects** of projects (definition, design, plans, milestones, cost, risk, procurement) as well as the **soft** aspects (motivation, skills, stakeholders, change management, communication)
- **Where**: the **organization**, the **culture**, the **priorities** and the **context** (internal and external) in which the project is being carried out.

All of the details will be explained in chapter five.

I hope you enjoy and learn from reading this book.

MY PROJECT LIFE

WE MEASURE OUR LIVES IN
PROJECTS. BUT WHAT HAVE I
LEARNED FROM MY GLOBAL
PROJECT LIFE?

I have been researching, leading and working on projects for the past 25 years. It has been a series of ups and downs, trial and error, doubts and convictions, false starts and occasionally great endings.

My career started at Unisys, a global information technology company, working as an order entry analyst. My day-to-day job was a set of routine tasks: processing client orders, ensuring that the mainframes were produced by the factories and monitoring the delivery process. Six months into the job, I was invited to be part of a strategic project: the set-up of a shared service centre (SSC) for Europe, the Middle East and Africa. The project goals were to reduce costs and improve the quality of services by consolidating all back office and administrative activities in one central location, Amsterdam. The only caveat my boss told me was that "you have to do it in addition to your order entry responsibilities".

I quickly became bored with the order entry work but loved being part of the project, especially the challenge of creating something new that was going to bring so many benefits to my company. Yet, I quickly realized there was a problem: my day-to-day job was the priority for my bosses. It was frustrating to see how the project-related work was repeatedly delayed and pushed back. The implementation of the SSC was delayed by more than a year, but that didn't seem to matter.

It was a very valuable first lesson: **when there are trade-offs to be made between day-to-day and project work, the first one will always take priority**. It took me years to understand the 'why' of this dichotomy and the friction, or contradiction, between two different sets of tasks. I later called these 'running the business' versus 'changing the business', concepts that I covered extensively in my book *The Focused Organization*.[14] Academics call this organizational ambidexterity.[15]

After two years, I left Unisys and joined Price Waterhouse (PW) as a junior consultant. After my second day in the office, I was sent to one of the biggest consulting projects PW was carrying out at the time: the SAP ERP (enterprise resource planning) implementation at one of the largest petroleum and petrochemical enterprises in the world. I was surprised to see so many consultants working on a project. There must have been more than 30 of them, including SAP developers. I was assigned a role in the Project Support Office, which was in charge of the administrative side of the project. My first task was to chase project team members to fill in their timesheets so that PW could invoice the customer. No one instantly becomes the CEO and this was certainly a very lowly rung on the organizational ladder. Despite the large amount of resources dedicated to the initiative and the application of a well-defined project management methodology, the project was running two years late. The number of problems was daunting despite a fully dedicated team. I learned my second valuable lesson: **IT and technology projects are different – traditional project management methods don't seem to work.**

After that I worked on euro conversion and projects relating to the Year 2000 (Y2K) bugs. The thing that struck me most was that both of these types of project had a very high priority on the agenda of the executive teams. Large amounts of resources were dedicated to them, both internally and externally. Internal resources were allocated to work on the projects full time, something I had not seen before. Executive teams were highly engaged with these projects, following them closely and playing an active role. The plans included extensive testing and contingency planning. As opposed to my previous projects, these high-impact, complex projects were all delivered with precision, right on time.

While working as a consultant at PW, I experienced the first of four large mergers, when it joined forces with Coopers & Lybrand. This created PricewaterhouseCoopers (PwC), one of the largest audit and consulting firms in the world.

As a junior, you don't really know what the implications of such a merger can be. At first, it all sounds great. It is sold by the executives as a fantastic move, something that will be beneficial for both companies. However, with the experience of many mergers, I now realize there is a loser and a winner. Always.

Mergers are a particular kind of project, very different from those I had previously experienced, yet one of the most common strategic projects in the business world. Mergers trigger hundreds of projects aimed at integrating the two companies. They often require an integration office that monitors the successful execution of all the projects. I quickly realized that mergers and acquisitions (M&A) projects get lots of attention from executive teams, but mostly at the beginning, when the deal is announced. What makes these projects unique is that when the integration projects start, strong resistance materializes. It is a major force pushing the integration towards failure. The result is that many M&A projects hit the corporate buffers, mostly at the integration stage. According to research from *Harvard Business Review* and KMPG, between 70% and 90% of mergers fail to create any value.[16]

What struck me with the PwC merger was that most of the employees, from both firms, didn't want to merge. They didn't see the value of the change and preferred to stay as they were. And, despite this being considered a successful merger, several years later people were still talking about the good old times: "PW was much better, a truly global firm, while Coopers was a bunch of locals." I learned another lesson: **in projects, there is always a human and behavioural component that should be addressed. In the case of a merger, these aspects are critical and can take years to overcome. Doing nothing is not an option; the force can be so strong that it takes the project down.**

My last years at PwC saw my interest in projects increase and become my area of focus. It was obvious that managing a single project was always a complex endeavour. But organizations were running hundreds of them at the same time. The chaos and waste in this field were enormous, and the room for improvement was unlimited. It was 2003, and I decided to research the matter in detail. With the support of one partner, we launched the first ever piece of global research into project and programme management.

My first goal was to understand whether there is a correlation between good project management practices and successful project performance. The second was to learn what the best-in-class organizations were doing. The research covered some 64 countries and more than 200 companies. My paper *Boosting Business Performance through Programme and Project Management*[17] was a first in the project management world. It confirmed my assumptions and was considered an eye opener for many experts in the field. I was appointed PwC's Global Lead Practitioner in Project and Change Management.

After ten years with the firm, I had become a senior manager and was very close to becoming a partner – the promised land! The structure in a partnership has a pyramid shape, with junior consultants at the bottom and a very select well-remunerated few (the partners) at the top. The career path in these organizations is clear for everyone: either you meet the criteria to advance to the next level or you are out. To become a partner, you need to have a business plan, an idea that you develop into a business. If the partners believe that your idea would generate revenues of around $1 million per annum or more, they will invest in it and provide the resources to start the business.

I wanted to become a partner and my business idea was clear: to establish a project management advisory practice for PwC. I was convinced, and my research had shown, that every organization in the world needed to develop and improve its project delivery capabilities. The business case was crystal clear. After presenting it to the partners, I partied all night long, convinced that I was going to become a partner. The day after, first thing in the morning, at 8.46am, I was called in by PwC's managing partner to receive the good news. I still remember his exact words: "Antonio, we loved your presentation – we could see your passion and your global mastery of the subject. But, unfortunately, we don't believe in your idea. We think projects are something tactical, for IT or engineers. We cannot enter into that low-level field – we don't believe project competencies are something strategic." And then he continued: "With tremendous regret, Antonio, you are fired!"

It was 2006 and a turning point in my career. Should I move into a more traditional job, such as marketing, sales, accounting, finance or strategy? Or should I continue to work on my passion: projects? And another big question was wedged in my mind: **how can smart, highly educated and experienced leaders not appreciate the value of projects and project management?**

After lots of internal debate, I decided to focus on my passion and core expertise, which I had developed over the past ten years through multiple client assignments and two global research projects.

But, not only that, I decided to launch a personal quest, which was shared by all the project managers I had spoken to during my years of research and work in the field:

- First, I wanted to understand why senior executives, business media and academia had ignored projects as a key strategic element in organizations.
- Second, I was determined to change the overall thinking and bring projects to a strategic level in organizations, governments and schools. That would be my legacy.

After a few weeks, I was hired by Fortis Bank as Head of Post-Merger Integration. Fortis was a Belgian financial company active in insurance, banking and investment management. When I joined in 2007, Fortis was the 20th largest bank in the world by revenue.[18] The CEO, Jean-Paul Votron, who had joined in 2004, had set extremely ambitious plans for Fortis, which he wanted to transform into one of the top global players.

My role was focused on projects – lots of projects. After a company is acquired, the integration phase kicks in. I had to define the integration strategy and integration plans for the various business units, customer segments, regions, employees, organigrams, products, processes and systems. Usually the first 100 days are critical, and by the tenth day most of the important decisions have been made. As in the past, I noticed that M&A projects were treated differently from most of the other projects, because they were:

- considered of strategic importance
- high on the agenda of the executives
- well defined, with costs and benefits precisely estimated after thorough due diligence
- receiving lots of dedicated resources, both internal and external
- surrounded by communication, especially after the deal was signed
- establishing strong governance to monitor and support the integration.

In late 2007, in line with the CEO's ambitions to achieve exponential growth, Fortis was offered the chance to join a consortium formed by two other banks – Royal Bank of Scotland (RBS) and Banco Santander – to bid for the largest bank in the Netherlands, ABN AMRO, paving the way for the largest ever bank takeover in history. ABN AMRO was to be split amongst the three consortium partners, Fortis would get the retail and business activities in Benelux and the international investment company; integration of the retail activities into Fortis was subject to permission from De Nederlandsche Bank.

It was a once-in-a-career opportunity – a project that it was impossible to say no to. Despite the high risk of the deal, on 6 August 2007, over 90% of votes at the Fortis shareholder meetings in Brussels and the Dutch city of Utrecht backed both Fortis's proposed bid, one of Europe's largest ever.[19] Despite Fortis's investment of €24 billion (of the €71.9 billion that the transaction cost), the business case was compelling, and not just in terms of the financial aspects; the vision of becoming Europe's fifth-largest bank was inspirational.

For the first time in my career, I experienced a project where it felt like we were making history. This was something unique that had never been done before. Being part of the winning team was a huge morale boost for me and everyone.

Right after the deal was signed, I was sent to the ABN AMRO head-quarters in Amsterdam to set up the integration office and work on the approach, strategy and plans. But this time I was confronted with a new challenge: culture. The Dutch culture dominated at ABN AMRO, the Scottish at RBS, the Spanish at Banco Santander and the Belgian at Fortis. In addition, all had strong company cultures as well as their national cultures. RBS had a top-down, no nonsense approach; Banco Santander focused on value creation for themselves; ABN AMRO's people believed they were better but had been badly led; and Fortis focused on consensus and getting people to work together. You can see the difficulties. Apart from Fortis, the other three companies all wanted to be in the lead. Even ABN AMRO, which had just been acquired, often seemed to be in control and trying to make key decisions.

The project was one of the most intense times in my career. I worked very long hours, from 7am to 10pm, for about a year. Yet, I really enjoyed it and looked forward to getting back into it after the weekends. It was a unique, historical and strategic project, never done before. The 100 or more Fortis staff in Amsterdam were very close and united. All played a role and supported each other when needed. For the first time, I was part of a truly high-performing team working to make a dream a reality.

Despite the hard work, the financial crisis hit Fortis hard. On the late afternoon of Friday 26 September 2008, at the ABN AMRO bank, out of nowhere we were given boxes to put all our belongings in. What a shock!

Fortis had taken too many risks and invested in too many strategic projects at the same time. It was spread too thinly. Very few people knew the severity of the crisis. We learned the news through the radio and the press: **it was a lesson in disastrous project selection and portfolio management, and complete absence of communication, also known as a lack of transparency.**

My colleagues and I rented several vans, put our boxes inside and drove to Fortis NL, the bank's Dutch subsidiary, located just outside Amsterdam. After that we were allowed to go home for the weekend. We were told further information would be provided by the top management on Monday. As you can you imagine, the lack of information and clarity about what was happening, and the likely consequences for us all, occupied our minds constantly throughout the weekend. On Monday, we went to work at the Fortis NL offices. We continued working as if nothing had happened. The promised clarifications from top management never arrived. Even worse, on the following Friday, suddenly we were asked to pack all our belongings again and go back to Brussels. The Belgian government had bailed out the bank, and Fortis NL, together with ABN AMRO, had been given to the Dutch authorities. A second shock!

There was a general state of shock in the country too: Fortis was the largest company in Belgium, and almost every household knew someone who worked there or who had shares in the bank.

It took me a while to understand and digest what had happened so abruptly. The entire project, the one that we had been working so hard on for a year, vanished in a couple of weeks.

When the team arrived in Brussels, nobody really knew what had happened and what we had to do. The entire company was in a state of confusion, as if it had been hit by a speeding train. We were eagerly waiting for information and clarification, but it never came. I spent a year without a position yet still employed by the bank. Luckily, during this period there were no intentions to lay off employees.

Fortis was in the press every day, and employees who a few months before had been proud to say where they worked were now partially blamed for the collapse. During the bailout by the Belgian government, Fortis spent more than six months without a leader, without a vision, without a strategy. There was a strange void in the organization. The morale of the employees, many in states of bewilderment or depression, continued to deteriorate.

The takeover project brought Fortis close to bankruptcy. **It shows the importance of timing and context in decision making.**

On 12 May 2009, after several legal clashes and under immense social pressure, the Belgian government and the remaining shareholders approved the sale of Fortis to BNP Paribas. This leading French bank is well known for its risk-averse culture and patience in acquiring banks on the verge of liquidation.

The integration of Fortis into BNP Paribas was a state-of-the-art project. The global CFO of BNP Paribas Group, Jean-Laurent Bonnafé, was appointed CEO of BNP Paribas Fortis. He was sent to Brussels with a three-year mandate. It was one of the rare occasions that I saw a project sponsor, the top executive of a company, being fully dedicated to a project. His only goal was clear – to integrate Fortis with BNP Paribas – and everybody knew it. A characteristic of the project, as with most M&A initiatives, was that the total integration costs and benefits (synergies) were estimated with precision and communicated openly to the market. Resources were fully dedicated to the integration project. Internal people were excused from their day-to-day jobs to focus solely on the integration. A large number of high-end consultants were also engaged to accelerate the change and put pressure on the organization. The discipline injected was extraordinary. There were processes to be followed to define plans and key milestones, to estimate costs and savings, to design the new organization, and so on. There were no exceptions. Everyone, including the various leaders of the retail, private, wholesale banking businesses, had to comply with the new ways of working. Any resistance or non-compliance led to immediate consequences. With all these elements in place, it was obvious that the project would be successful.

I played a secondary role in the integration, close enough to understand how the project was being run but without any major responsibility. A year into the integration, the recommendation was made to establish a central office that would take care of overseeing projects. This would offer the perfect role for me, and it was another project in my career. I was appointed Head of Transversal Portfolio Management. My main responsibility was to support the BNP Paribas Fortis executive team in the selection, prioritization and monitoring of the implementation of all the projects in the bank. The office and the position were new. I had to start from scratch. The novelty of the office and position also highlighted that projects in the past had been like free atoms, running across the bank without any formal control or any standard way of managing them.

It was an eye-opening period. I had the opportunity to try what the books and experts were preaching in courses and conferences: projects should always be linked to a strategic objective; prioritization should apply a weighted formula of quantitative and qualitative benefits; senior management should choose the projects that will bring the most value to the organization; and so on.

Inevitably, the reality was different. Obtaining reliable data is one of the first challenges when trying to produce an overview of an organization's projects. Operational data, supply chain data, sales data and HR data are abundant and mostly accurate, thanks to the huge investment in ERP (enterprise resource planning) and CRM (customer relationship management) systems that organizations went through in the 1990s. But project data had not been treated in the same way. ERP covers some of the financial aspects of projects, but that is about it. It took me and my team almost six months to collect reliable and accurate project information so as to be able to do the analysis required by the bank's management.

One of the key findings of the analysis presented to the first executive project review committee was that the bank had been investing in too many cost-reduction (74%) and compliance (22%) projects, while almost no projects were aimed at growing the business (4%). The first comment was: "*How is it possible, we bring all the money to the bank, but we don't receive any budget for our projects?*" The Executive Committee agreed that going forward, we would aim at a more balanced portfolio of projects, and that for the next two years, we would favour growth projects.

In addition to the project mix, there was a listing with all the large projects that the bank was running, together with potential new ones. For the first time in the bank's history, all the key projects could be seen on one slide. The list had a very clear red line, which was where the budget allocated to projects (€100 million) stopped. The projects below the red line had to be stopped, delayed or not started. There was a long silence in the room as everyone looked at the list of projects below the red line. Their faces turned sour when they realized that I was proposing to cancel some of their projects. They tried to justify all of the projects below the line: this one is really important for our business; I know someone working on this one; this one can't be cancelled – we've been working on it for the past four years; and so on. Sound familiar?

Interestingly, the top executives of the bank had never been asked to choose, or to cancel, projects. In the past, every idea had triggered a new project, and there had been no initial constraints.

Despite the hard work in collecting the information and the surprise the analysis caused, once the executives had digested the tough discussions and decisions, the feedback was extremely positive; receiving praise from the Executive Committee members. They acknowledged that it was one of the first times they had a focused, constructive and transparent discussion around the long-term strategy of the bank.

Even if it was a very tough period, it was one of the richest learning experiences in my career.

As I mentioned, during the turbulent transition period between the collapse of Fortis and the official takeover by BNP Paribas, I decided to start working on one of my dreams: writing a book. It was an idea that I had had in mind since my time at PwC. **Writing a book is a project, and the first time you write a book, it's a project that doesn't go according to plan. Like every personal project, it has a lot to do with your own discipline and the way you prioritize your limited time.**

A big part of my book was researching and understanding why I had been fired from PwC, and why senior leaders didn't understand or appreciate the strategic value of projects and project management. My research shed some light on the matter. First, I found that business schools ignored project management. Out of the top 100 MBA programmes in the world, only two taught project management as a full mandatory course. Second, large business media, such as *Harvard Business Review*, didn't publish much about projects and how to successfully execute them. I discovered that, between 1972 and 2012, *Harvard Business Review* had published 4,750 articles on marketing, 4,324 on finance and 4,313 on strategy, to a meagre 299 on project management. Third, top consulting firms, such as McKinsey, didn't offer any advice on how to improve project execution or implementation practices. Project management was not taught, published or consulted upon by the most strategic organizations. Very few leaders or CEOs had any exposure to the art and science of projects. With the name of my book – *The Focused Organization: How Concentrating on a Few Key Initiatives Can Dramatically Improve Strategy Execution*[20] – I wanted to highlight the importance of projects in successful strategy implementation.

During my two years of research (spanning 2009 to 2011), I first identified the gradual shift in the way organizations were performing their work and allocating their resources. There had been a slow but steady move – of resources, budgets and focus – from day-to-day activities to projects. Since then, the shift has accelerated exponentially, to the point that in a few years most of the work carried out will be done through projects.

I also discovered that one of the reasons project management was ignored was partially due to the way the founders of the modern project management defined it in the 1970s. The methodology and standards focused primarily on inputs, tools, deliverables, control and documentation instead of highlighting the impact, value and benefits provided to the organization, to clients, to citizens, to the region or to the world. The language and terms applied were too technical and far from mainstream business language. No wonder most leaders saw project management as technical and tactical instead of a strategic competency – a way of working that creates significant value. One of the main purposes of this book is to resolve this matter: to make project management simpler to understand and to apply, and to provide the skills, tools and mindset for everyone to excel in their projects and turn their dreams into reality.

One of the last important steps in my career was joining the Project Management Institute (PMI) as a volunteer. Founded in 1969, PMI is the world-leading project management association. It provides the most recognized project management standard (the Project Management Body of Knowledge, or PMBOK) and certification (Project Management Professional, or PMP). In July 2018, PMI had more than 800,000 active credential holders and more than 500,000 members across nearly every country in the world.

I thought that there could not be a better way to influence the world of projects than from a leadership position within PMI. I imagined that I could push PMI to go beyond its traditional boundaries: the World Economic Forum annual meeting in Davos, the Nobel Peace Prize … these were some of my most ambitious dreams.

I set myself the target of joining PMI's Board of Directors, which actually happened rather quickly. In 2013, I was elected by the members to represent them for six years. After several officer positions, I was appointed chairman of PMI in 2016. **My agenda was clear: to make sure** that leaders and key decision makers understand and appreciate the value of projects and project implementation. **Under my guidance, PMI launched the biggest initiative and investment in its almost 50-year history: the Brightline Initiative.**[21] This strategic undertaking has created a global coalition with leading organizations and has now gained the recognition of key influential forums such as Davos, *The Economist, Harvard Business Review*, Thinkers50, the Global Peter Drucker Forum and TED Talks. The project management awareness gap is being closed.

In 2015, I left BNP Paribas Fortis and joined GlaxoSmithKline Vaccines as director of the Global Project Management Office, the latest project in my career. Moving from banking to pharma is rather unusual. In fact, I found out that there were close to a hundred candidates for the position, many with years of pharma experience. But my strong focus on projects, and implementation, was a key differentiator in enabling me to get this very exciting and sought-after position.

After more than 20 years working in and promoting the value of projects and project management, 2017 was a year of extraordinary recognition: I was honoured to receive one of the most prestigious prizes in the management thinking world: the Thinkers50 Ideas into Practice award. The award recognized my work as the world's leading champion of project management and the founder of a global movement that has transformed the tactical topic of project management into one of the central issues in the CEO's 2020 agenda. Beyond my personal satisfaction, this was a recognition of the importance of projects and of the daily silent hard work and perseverance of millions of project managers, project leaders and project directors around the world.

An important final lesson from my career is that you should focus on your passion, your work and what you're really like. People around you will be sceptical, or even oppose what you are doing, but do not let them choose for you. As the old adage says, "Choose a job you love and you will never have to work a day in your life."

BUT WHAT IS A PROJECT?

ALWAYS BEGIN BY DEFINING WHAT EXACTLY A PROJECT INVOLVES. MEANING IS THE ROOT OF ACHIEVEMENT.

I have been lucky enough to spend some time with Roger Martin. Roger is, according to Thinkers50, the world's leading management thinker. A former dean of the Rotman School of Management in Canada, someone who has worked closely with the leaders of Procter & Gamble and LEGO, and a best-selling author, Roger is impressive and worth listening to. He argues that one of the problems today[22] is that careers and jobs are structured as if they are flat rather than spiky. In reality, they are filled with the peaks and troughs of projects. He says:

At least 80% and perhaps as high as 95% of jobs are an amalgam of projects. But instead of thinking, "My life is projects," the average person in an office building thinks that their life is some sort of regular job and that the projects get in the way of their regular job. And so projects are put off and mismanaged. In fact, in organizations the entire decision factory should be thought of as nothing but projects. Managers should organize their lives around projects. They should look more like professional service firms.[23]

These thoughts are echoed throughout the corporate world. Projects are routinely marginalized. Regularly, when I start exploring why companies have so many projects and why they often fail in delivering them or achieving any tangible benefits, to the point that a senior executive told me once: *"If you want to make sure that something is not done, make it a project."*

Over the years, I have found that the word 'project' is extensively used yet largely misunderstood in today's private and public sectors. This phenomenon generates two issues that have an impact on the success rate of project delivery.

The first issue is of definition: many activities that were traditionally performed in normal day-to-day time are now labelled projects. This exponentially increases the number of projects and project managers in an organization. Not long ago, I did some work for a leading biotech company. It had 80 staff and seven executives who had a list of more than 400 projects on top of their day-to-day activities. It was, of course, unmanageable and total chaos. And this disease affects almost every organization today, creating several kinds of collateral damage, one of them around prioritization, a topic I will address later in this book.

The second issue is increased bureaucracy and cost. If you apply project management techniques to all of your projects, you will be increasing complexity, growing costs and creating extra governance committees for some undertakings that don't need it. As we will see in this chapter, project management is not 'for free'. On average, you should add 7% to 11% extra cost to the activity for the dedicated management, monitoring, reporting and extra governance.

When the English language initially adopted the word 'project', it referred to a plan of something, not to the act of carrying this plan out. The use expanded to include both the planning and the implementation phases in the 1950s, when several techniques for project management were introduced. In the late 1960s, several associations were founded around the practice of project management. Most notable were the International Project Management Association (IPMA) in Vienna, founded in 1965, and the Project Management Institute (PMI) in Philadelphia, established in 1969. One of their initial aims was to outline common definitions and best practices.

PMI's definition of a project is as follows:

A **project** is temporary in that it has a defined beginning and end in time, and therefore defined scope and resources. And a project is unique in that it is not a routine operation, but a specific set of operations designed to accomplish a singular goal. So a project team often includes people who don't usually work together – sometimes from different organizations and across multiple geographies. The development of software for an improved business process, the construction of a building or bridge, the relief effort after a natural disaster, the expansion of sales into a new geographic market – all are projects. And all must be expertly managed to deliver the on-time, on-budget results, learning and integration that organizations need.[24]

Other formal definitions of a project are:
- "A project is a unique set of processes consisting of coordinated and controlled activities with start and finish dates, undertaken to achieve an objective. Achievement of the project objective requires deliverables conforming to specific requirements including

multiple constraints such as time, cost and resources" (ISO 21500 Guidance on project management).[25]

- "A project is a managed set of interrelated resources that delivers one or more products to a customer or end user. The set of resources has a definite beginning and end and operates according to a plan" (Software Engineering Institute).[26]
- "A project is a time and cost constrained operation to realize a set of defined deliverables (the scope to fulfil the project's objectives) up to quality standards and requirements" (International Project Management Association).[27]
- "A temporary organization that is created for the purpose of delivering one or more business products according to a specified Business Case" (Office of Government Commerce UK).[28]
- "A project is a unique, transient endeavour undertaken to achieve planned objectives" (Association for Project Management).[29]

As you have probably noticed, most of the official definitions tend to be quite technical, wordy and difficult to understand for the non-advanced individual. This partly explains why project management has largely been considered a technical and tactical practice, far from the strategic themes in management and leadership.

My own definition aims to develop a universal common understanding:

A project is a **proven method of bringing ideas into reality**. It has a purpose, aiming at solving a problem or creating something new. It is unique by nature – even if it has been done before, some elements will be different. A project (often) requires a team of mixed skills and expertise and demands a project leader to drive the team. It is constrained by time (has an end date or finish line), budget (funds and resources) and design (ambition and quality). A project has to address – often through intensive communication – individual, collective and cultural behaviours (stakeholders).

It is also helpful to understand how projects differ from operations and day-to-day activities:

- Projects are one-off investments designed to achieve predetermined objectives, whereas operations are day-to-day activities with similar objectives every year (with some marginal improvements).
- Projects are restricted in terms of time and budget and are staffed with temporary team members. In contrast, operations are repetitive, can be more easily automated, operate according to a yearly budget and are staffed with full-time team members.
- Projects need different types of resources and competencies than do operations. Project leaders tend to be more generalist, and they need to work transversely to bring different views together and thus require diplomacy and negotiation skills. They also need to be good at managing uncertainty, because large strategic projects are not predictable from one week to another. In contrast, operations resources tend to be highly technical and experts in their part of the business. They master areas such as finance, marketing or operations.

AND PROJECT MANAGEMENT?

Part art, part science, project management is the practice of delivering projects successfully.

The term 'project management' that is in use today emerged in the second half of the 20th century, mostly after the Second World War. Prior to then, projects were managed on an ad hoc basis, mostly using informal techniques and tools.[30] The unprecedented period of abundant reconstruction projects in the post-war period required the organization of vast quantities of resources to achieve objectives by established deadlines. Governments started to request companies to be more precise on their plan and cost estimates. All these megaprojects required a comprehensive approach, beyond following intuitive processes.

Henry Gantt (1861–1919) is considered one of the founding fathers of modern project management. He created the scheduling diagram known as the Gantt chart, used to visualize the key steps of a project on a timeline. It was used in some of the most iconic infrastructure projects in the 1930s, like the Hoover Dam and the Manhattan projects. Today, it has become an essential part of every project manager's toolkit.

After the second world war, organizations started to apply methodical approaches, tools and techniques to better control and plan complex projects. The US Navy and some consulting firms, like Booz Allen Hamilton, were some of the first contributors in developing modern project management. This started to be seen as a discipline different from engineering or architecture.

The big focus those early years of project management was about accuracy of estimations and planning (scheduling). Two of the most important advances were formulas around these areas. The first one was the program evaluation and review technique (PERT), developed by Booz Allen Hamilton, used for advance estimation. The second was the 'critical path method' created by two corporations, DuPont and the Remington Rand, to improve the planning and controlling of the projects.

This strong focus on the inputs – planning, estimation, cost, time, scope, risk management – of projects remained the essence of modern project management until our times. The outputs – concepts such as purpose, rationale, value, benefits, impact, strategy and customers – were not part of the initial definitions of project management. This oversight is one of the main reasons why the discipline of project management grew apart from the mainstream management, leadership and strategic themes that dictated the CEO agenda over the past 30 years.

Like the above definitions of projects, definitions of project management are rather cumbersome and hard to understand by the normal person. To keep things simple, I prefer to refer to **project management as the competencies, techniques and tools that help people to define, plan and implement projects successfully.**

However, there are two additional elements of this concept that I would like to highlight.

First, and as mentioned earlier, **project management has a cost**. Always. It adds a layer of overhead and oversight to the implementation of a number of activities. It requires resources and time (in the form of extra meetings) for an organization, which similarly have a cost. According to studies, the project management costs for all phases of a project generally total somewhere between 7% and 11% of the project's total cost.[31] If additional project controls are added, such as external audits, project management costs will be in the 9% to 15% range.[32] Project managers of small projects usually end up doing some of the project work and will have difficulty adhering solely to the project management role, but costs should be held to a minimum. A larger degree of project management can be justified for medium-sized projects, and the largest amount of project management should be applied to large projects, where the stakes rise along with the project's complexity and risk.

In an organization, it is important to set some clear and objective criteria for what a project is and, in contrast, what should be considered day-to-day activities (or what I call 'running the business'). Here as well there are different theories, yet I tend to be very pragmatic as often there is no black-and-white answer in what we do. I recommend defining a set of criteria, such as:

- size of the project in terms of budget (e.g. above 500,000 dollars or euros)
- size in terms of duration (e.g. between 6 and 24 months)
- more than five fully dedicated resources or full-time equivalents
- at least three units, departments and/or regions impacted
- linked to a strategic objective.

Projects that comply with these as a minimum three of these criteria should be managed by professional project managers using project management processes, tools and techniques, including risk management. They will also require setting up the right governance structure and monitoring mechanism to ensure the project is well executed.

The biotech company I mentioned above set some basic definitions (in this case, projects would be initiatives that required more than 500 man-days and at least €400,000 investment, and that were of a transversal nature). The company was able to reduce its list of key projects from 400 to 25, which we then prioritized and staffed properly, significantly improving the projects' implementation.

There are two key takeaways here that you should consider when looking at your list of projects:

- Classify as projects only those that meet certain criteria.
- Apply project management when the size and complexity of the project require it.

The second additional element to bear in mind is that **project management is moving to project leadership**. Over the past 30 years, there has been a steady shift in focus from the hard technical elements of projects and project management (such as scheduling, scoping, finance and risks) to the softer elements (such as people, behaviour, culture, communication and change). We will see later the skills required to implement a project, but the leadership part is becoming more relevant and needed than the management.

HOW PROJECTS EVOLVED

To put the definition of projects and the evolving art of project management in context, it is useful to consider the evolution of projects. If we look at the definition, we can conclude that projects have been an integral part of human nature since the origins of humankind. Today's project management is the result of a natural process of evolution and has been practised throughout the history of humanity.

Hunting for food could be considered as one of the first human project-based activities. Going out to catch food for the family and the village was an activity with time and resource constraints, full of risks and with stakeholders expecting a result. Once hunting became more regular and the techniques had been mastered, the activity moved from a project to a routine activity. The establishment of the first villages, the first castles, the first irrigation systems, the wheel – all these were new ideas that were made reality through a project mentality that was perfected over time by introducing new techniques and learning from past mistakes.

Symbolically, there are two major projects considered as the first megaprojects in history. The first is the construction of the Great Wall of China, built between 250 BC and AD 1450 as protection against invading Mongolian forces and other nomadic groups. The stone walls span over 6,000 kilometres and it remains the longest structure ever built.

The second is the great Pyramid of Giza (finished around 2560 BC), constructed in only 20 years with the goal of serving as the tomb of the Pharaoh. It was made from 2.3 million limestone blocks, which were sourced and lifted by human hands from over 800 kilometres away. The pyramid remained the tallest human-made structure in the world for over 3,800 years, unsurpassed until the 160-metre-tall spire of Lincoln Cathedral was completed in around 1300.

Other ancient projects that have survived the age of time and have become landmarks are:

- The **city of Teotihuacan in Mexico** was built between the 1st and 7th centuries AD. At its peak in AD 450, it had a population of 200,000, making it one of the largest cities in the world at that time.
- The **Colosseum in Rome**, constructed between AD 70 and 80, was the largest amphitheatre ever built.
- The **Hagia Sophia in Istanbul**, completed in approximately six years in the 6th century AD, it is considered the most important Byzantine monument and remained the largest Christian church in the world for nearly 1,000 years.
- **Machu Picchu in Peru**, also known as the Lost City of the Incas, is a pre-Columbian Inca site built for the Emperor Pachacuti around AD 1450.
- The **Taj Mahal in India**, built by the Fifth Mughal Emperor, Shah Jahan, as a tribute to his favourite wife, Mumtaz Mahal. It was built between AD 1631 to 1653 and employed approximately 20,000 artisans and craftsmen.
- The many **cathedrals** that have survived to modern times are also historic projects, St Peter's Basilica in the Vatican being one of the most famous. Interestingly, as opposed to some of the other buildings, some cathedrals took centuries to build, being worked on by generations of builders, sculptors, architects and so on. Two main factors explain the duration of these **projects that last centuries**: the lack of public funds and the evolving design (scope) of the cathedrals, whose styles changed (Romanesque, Gothic, Renaissance, Baroque etc.) while the construction was ongoing. A notorious project is the Sagrada Familia in Barcelona, which was started in 1882 and is expected to be completed in 2026,

a century after the death of its original architect, Antoni Gaudi. It is said that when some of the leading architects of cathedrals were challenged about the long delays their projects were experiencing, they claimed that "God is not in a rush."

These remarkable creations were designed and created by engineers, architects and craftspeople. Yet, to be successful, they applied project management principles and concepts similar to the ones used today. Their overseers had to manage and motivate thousands of workers for many years, ensure that there was enough funding to purchase the materials and pay the workers, and communicate regularly with the chief, leader or commander to ensure their expectations were met. They didn't have unlimited budgets, they didn't have unlimited resources and they didn't have unlimited time. They were also extremely focused on quality, to ensure that the construction was of sufficient quality to resist wars and natural disasters. Without a good understanding of all of these principles, these projects would never have succeeded.

Mark Kozak-Holland, in his book *The History of Project Management*,[33] corroborates that project management is not just a 20th and 21st century discipline. However, despite the enormous number of historical projects, the documentation and historical records are scarce. This can be attributed to a combination of factors. First, the initiators of the projects were generally more interested in their outcome than in their methodology in terms of planning and implementation. Second, the people responsible for creating these buildings were craftsmen, who were not necessarily educated or interested in making their methods known to others. On the contrary, in many of these projects, the details of their execution were kept a secret among a certain tribe or family who specialized in a certain branch of craftsmanship and transmitted their knowledge from one generation to another.

The next generation of projects were large civil engineering projects, such as dams, bridges, tunnels and highways. Next came large emblematic projects such as concert houses (e.g. Sydney Opera House), sport stadiums (e.g. the stadiums and other facilities built for the Sochi Winter and Beijing Summer Olympics), museums (e.g. the Guggenheim) and skyscrapers. From the Empire State Building in New York to the Burj Khalifa in Dubai, projects have always been used to stretch the limits of nature and human achievements.

The greatest governments and political leaders have been big promoters of projects. Some of them have embraced projects to develop their regions and countries with the aim of crafting and implementing a long-term vision (e.g. in Singapore, Shenzhen, Taiwan and Dubai). Others have used projects to bring their countries out of a recession or even out of war (e.g. in Iceland, Rwanda and Argentina).

Nowadays, we talk about 'megaprojects'[34] – projects with a budget of more than \$1 billion[35] that attract significant public attention due to their substantial impact on communities, environment and budgets. Examples of megaprojects include railways, airports, seaports, power plants, oil and natural gas extraction projects, public buildings, aerospace projects and smart cities. Their numbers have become ever larger, but the fundamental truths of projects and how best to manage them remain the same.

GETTING PROJECTS RIGHT

PROJECTS FREQUENTLY FAIL,
SOMETIMES SPECTACULARLY.
SO, WHAT ARE THE MOST COMMON
STUMBLING BLOCKS AND HOW
CAN THEY BE AVOIDED?

Imagine a world in which most projects – personal, social, corporate, organizational and governmental – are successfully accomplished. That is my purpose, and the reason for writing this book.

There is work to be done. Only a select few projects deliver their purpose, meet their expected goals, achieve sustainable benefits, satisfy most stakeholders, meet their deadlines and stay within their original financial budget. So what is the secret? What can we learn from the thousands of failed projects? And how can we develop a framework or tool that guarantees, or at least significantly increases the chance of project success?

First, we need to pay attention to projects as never before and equip people for the revolution. We need to arm people with the tools and techniques they need to survive in the project-driven world. Research proves that very few people receive an education that teaches them the tools and techniques needed to define and manage projects successfully.[36] As I will explain in chapter eight, the leading business schools in the world, such as Harvard, MIT, Wharton, Stanford, IMD, INSEAD and the London Business School, don't teach project management as part of the core curriculums of their MBA programmes. For decades, project management competencies have been considered tactical and irrelevant for senior roles in organizations. The world is led by strategy, finance, marketing and sales experts.

Second, we need to recalibrate organizations by allocating more power, resources and budgets to project-based work. All organizations need to take note.

Efficiency gains in operational work started with mass production more than 100 years ago, and the trend has continued progressively since. Fewer resources have been dedicated to operational work year after year. Since the 1920s, or even before, companies have been improving their operations (which in my previous book, *The Focused Organization*, I renamed 'running the business') as a means of becoming more efficient and reducing costs. At that time, most companies were mainly producing goods – the service industry was not yet strong – and one of their main objectives was to grow. Growth by acquisition was not as popular as it is today. Growth was more organic, by increasing production capacity and by entering new markets. Once the industries became more mature, growth was achieved by increasing efficiencies and reducing costs. The impact of these growth techniques was that the number of projects ('changing the business') increased over time.

To understand this trend, we need to look at the evolution of the economy. Governments' and central banks' economic and monetary structures have a direct impact on the number of projects that organizations can run. The amount of money in circulation in the economy, the availability of 'cheap' money (i.e. low interest rates) and the velocity of the money (i.e. the average frequency with which a unit of money is spent) can be indicators of this shift. The more money there is in the economy, the more companies use it to invest in strategic projects. The lower the interest rates, the more companies borrow to invest in strategic projects. To explain this, we can look at the evolution of gross domestic product (GDP) over the past century in the UK,[37] making the following assumptions:

- In recession years (negative GDP), companies reduce their spending on projects.
- In years with no GDP growth, nothing changes.
- In years with growth (positive GDP), companies increase their spending on projects.

The impact of these increases or decreases is felt the following year. FIGURE 2 shows the results of this analysis.

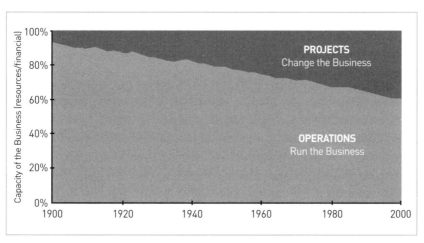

FIGURE 2.

Shift from day-to-day work (operations) to change activities (projects)

An important element that significantly influenced this trend was the fact that almost all the management thinkers and their management theories focused on improvements for the 'run the business' dimension. Key management influencers, such as Frederick Taylor, Henry Ford, W. Edwards Deming, Igor Ansoff and Michael Porter, focused their recommendations on improving the operations of the business. Ironically perhaps, these operational improvements were carried out as projects. These were often one-off projects, but changing a business involves carrying out a project; there is no other way.

As well as management thinking, several other movements have helped to accelerate this trend:

- in the 1970s, the universalization of the PC at work
- in the 1980s, the business process reengineering wave
- in the 1990s, enterprise resource planning (ERP) to automate most operations
- in the 2000s, the outsourcing of core and supporting operations
- in the 2010s, big data and extreme automation.

The result of all of these changes is that companies have made their operations extremely efficient, reaching levels where finding additional efficiency improvements is no longer possible. At the same time, the number of projects in organizations, the amount of resources dedicated to them and the size of projects have all increased year after year. Projects are on the march and established organizational and management models are under threat as never before.

Yet, according to my latest research, more is to come. Disruptive technologies will accelerate this trend. Robots and artificial intelligence will take over almost all the traditional administrative activities and operational work. Some of these roles have already disappeared or been completely reshaped. Organizations will shift their focus more than ever to projects and project-based work. Projects are the new norm for creating value and, indeed, for staying in business – leading to what I describe as the Project Revolution.

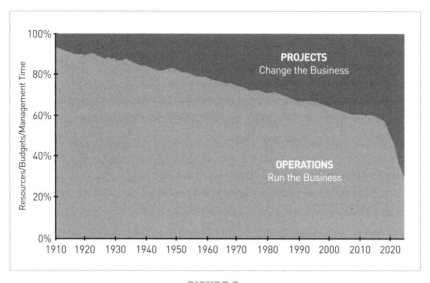

FIGURE 3.

Shift accelerated due to mass adoption of artificial
intelligence and robots in organizations

MOVING BEYOND EFFICIENCY

Moving beyond efficiency to change the business rather than simply
running the business is a difficult task. My experience and research
suggest that many organizations:

- lack information on how well they are implementing their projects
  and their overall strategy
- lack visibility about the number of projects they are running as
  well as those projects' status, actual cost, estimated completion
  cost, benefits and business case
- lack data about the status of their projects – status reports take
  weeks to produce and never show accurate information
- initiate projects without proper analysis and a clear business case
- continually increase the number of company-wide projects, with
  many more projects being started than completed
- have unclear ownership of many projects, including some of the
  most strategic ones

- don't have a cross-departmental governing body that decides in which projects to invest and ensures that projects are correctly executed
- display poor communication and collaboration between the business and functional departments
- simply don't have an integrated tool to manage projects
- suffer increasingly long lead times to develop and to launch new products to market.

Little wonder, perhaps, that many projects fail.

It is hard to know precisely how much money is wasted every year due to poor decision making, lack of competencies and inadequate understanding of the importance of sound project management practices. Several studies have tried to estimate the value destruction of this shortcoming in management. The facts are overwhelming:

- The 2018 Pulse of the Profession, a global survey conducted by the Project Management Institute (PMI), revealed around **$1 million is wasted every 20 seconds** collectively by organizations around the globe due to the ineffective implementation of business strategy through poor project management practices. This equates to roughly **$1.5 trillion wasted a year** – equivalent to the GDP of Brazil.[38]
- A study by the IT consultancy 6point6 based on a survey of 300 CIOs highlighted that businesses in the UK waste an estimated **£37 billion per year** on failed agile IT projects.[39]
- A study published by *Harvard Business Review* in 2011 analysed 1,471 IT projects and found that the **average overrun was 27%**, but one in six projects had a cost overrun of 200% on average and a schedule overrun of almost 70%.[40]
- Another study found that IT failure costs the US economy about **$50–150 billion annually**.[41] The same study claims that **roughly 30% of projects under US$1 billion fail to achieve the desired outcomes, and the rate rises to 50% for projects over US$1 billion**. This applies regardless of the country in which a project is constructed. Failure rates can be even higher in emerging markets and remote locations such as those found in Africa, where numerous risk factors, if not properly addressed, can combine to build a 'perfect storm' that derails a project.

- A study by PwC that reviewed 10,640 projects from 200 companies in 30 countries and across various industries found that **only 2.5% of the companies successfully completed 100% of their projects**.[42]
- McKinsey & Company studied over **5,000 projects and found that 56% delivered less value than expected**, 45% were over budget and 17% unfolded so badly that they threatened the company's very survival.[43]
- According to Gartner, **85% of big data projects fail** to move past preliminary stages.[44]
- A study published by the Association of Spanish Geographers estimates that between 1995 and 2016 **Spanish government agencies spent more than €81 billion on "infrastructure that was unnecessary, abandoned, underutilized or poorly programmed"**. And this figure could surpass €97 billion in the near future, factoring in the amounts that have already been pledged. The report says: "All of it was done without a proper cost/benefit analysis, and often on the basis of estimates of future users or earnings supported by a scenario of economic euphoria that was as evident as it was fleeting."[45]
- Massive cost overruns in **China's infrastructure investment** regime were highlighted by a scathing report from the University of Oxford's Saïd Business School. The report analysed 95 large Chinese road and rail transport projects and 806 transport projects built in rich democracies. "For over half of the infrastructure investments in China made in the last three decades, the costs are larger than the benefits they generate, which means the projects destroy economic value instead of generating it," the study said. Estimates from the Saïd Business School say the **cost overruns have set the nation back by some $28 trillion** – more than the combined GDPs of the US, Japan and Germany.[46]

If we look at individual project failures, the list is both appalling and never-ending. Some of the most notorious cases are:
- **International Space Station (ISS)**: This orbital laboratory is a joint effort between Russia, Europe, Japan, Canada and the US. The project was so complex and unwieldy that it was already four

years behind schedule when it began in 1998, and its original estimated cost of $17.4 billion ultimately grew to $150 billion. So far, the ISS hasn't been as much of a success as NASA hoped.[47]

- **Montreal Olympic Stadium (1976)**: This was originally nicknamed The Big O thanks to its name and shape but was later dubbed The Big Owe thanks to spiralling costs (a budget of $148 million vs a final cost $3.1 billion – more than 20 times the original budget). Despite the hard deadline, it wasn't actually completed on time after a manic push to complete the facility on time – work on major components such as the mast and retractable roof didn't begin until after the games. The Montreal Olympics left the city with a $1.6 billion debt.[48]

- **Sochi Winter Olympics (2014)**: The amount spent on the Winter Olympics was $51 billion in contrast to a $12 billion budget – much higher than the $40 billion spent by China on the 2008 Summer Olympics, which had three times the number of events. Most of Sochi's infrastructure projects, including the main stadium and other sporting venues to support the games, were built from scratch. A vast majority of projects ran catastrophically over budget, making this the costliest Olympic Games in history.[49]

- **Boston's Big Dig**: Boston's grand plan to bury the city's central highway in a 5.5-kilometre tunnel was budgeted to cost $2.8 billion but ended up costing $14.8 billion. Begun in 1982, it was plagued by escalating costs, overruns, leaks, accusations of shoddy workmanship and substandard materials, criminal arrests and a death. Originally scheduled to be completed in 1998, it was finally completed in 2007. The *Boston Globe* estimated that the project will ultimately cost $22 billion, including interest – and that it won't be paid off until 2038.[50]

- **Hoa Sen Group steel plant**: In April 2017, Vietnamese prime minister Nguyen Xuan Phuc halted work on this $10.6 billion, 4,200-acre steel plant to prevent a chemical spill. The Vietnamese government is determined not to grant licences to any projects with a high pollution risk.[51]

- **UK Electronic Health Records Project**: This is considered the world's largest civilian IT project. In 2011, after nine years of development work, UK government officials scrapped the £12 billion project, which had aimed at creating a unified electronic health records system for British citizens.[52]

- **The Channel Tunnel**: The idea of connecting the UK with mainland Europe had been there for centuries, but the project only started in 1988. Construction of the 51-kilometres tunnel took 6 years, one year longer than planned. The project total cost accounted to £4.6 billion, 80% over the initial budget (£2.6 billion). It is considered one of the most expensive construction projects in history. The project was funded privately, through bank loans and selling shares to the public. The original shareholders lost most of their money.[53]

- **Elbphilharmonie Hamburg**: This world-class concert hall project was launched with a forecasted price tag of €77 million and scheduled to open in 2010. Yet, the project was actually finished in 2016 and cost €789 million, ten times the original amount. It has been subject to a catalogue of disputes and lawsuits and a lengthy parliamentary inquiry.[54]

- **US Air Force ERP Project**: This initiative was seen as a solution to enable the Air Force to get its diverse technical systems to interact together nicely. Instead – after seven years and $1 billion spending – the project was abandoned in late 2012.[55]

- **Energiewende**: This is a German energy project aiming to transition away from fossil and nuclear energies (closing all nuclear power plants by 2022) and towards green energies. In reality, the country has not seen its emissions of greenhouse gases fall since 2009. German households, though, have to bear astronomical costs. One study estimates that the Energiewende project will cost Germans more than €1.5 trillion by 2050.[56]

- **Healthcare.gov**: The flagship website for the Affordable Care Act was supposed to give Americans a fast, easy way to enrol for health plans. Instead, on the opening day (1 October 2013), it collapsed and didn't meet the enrolment expectations. The estimated cost of the project's failure was $600 million.[57]

- **Desalination plants in Australia**: Almost $10 billion was invested in four big desalination plants in Sydney, Adelaide, Melbourne and Brisbane after a 12-year drought, the Millennium Drought, which ended in 2010. National authorities had launched an aggressive programme of desalination development in big coastal cities. The plants were ultimately so expensive to operate that they were closed down.[58]

- **Shell's Arctic drilling campaign closure**: In September 2015, Royal Dutch Shell pulled out of the Arctic after spending $7 billion and asserting that its Chukchi Sea offshore drilling project would yield world-class quantities of oil and natural gas. The company cited as reasons its fruitless effort to discover commercial quantities of fossil fuels, dangerous Arctic drilling conditions, rising expenses and civic protest.[59]

- **V. C. Summer nuclear power station**: One of two nuclear power projects under construction in South Carolina in the US was scrapped on 31 July 2017. Construction on the Westinghouse-designed, 2,200-megawatt-generating station started in 2013 and was scheduled to be completed by 2018 at a cost of $11.8 billion. Scana Corp. and South Carolina Electric and Gas, the plant's developers, stopped work after estimated completion costs ballooned to $25 billion and the construction schedule was extended well into the 2020s. The decision to halt the project came four months after Westinghouse declared bankruptcy and underscores the financial challenges facing US nuclear power.[60]

Similarly, shocking figures are easily found elsewhere. Look at start-up projects. Since its launch in 2009, Kickstarter, the leading crowdfunding platform for start-ups, has hosted more than 409,000 projects, raising more than $3.30 billion. About 147,000 of them, or 36%, have been successfully funded. However, according to Kickstarter's own statistics, **63.75% of start-up projects funded have failed.**[61]

And we are often not just talking about fiascos in terms of costs overruns or late delivery. It is even harder to quantify the losses in unmet benefits, social impact and revenues from the massive delays, or failures, caused by poor projects and deficient project leadership – let alone whether the initial estimated benefits were actually met.

The fact is that the world will see an increase in project spending – an average \$3.7 trillion[62] in annual infrastructure spending between now and 2035 to keep pace with expected GDP growth – yet, the risk of project failure will continue to be huge unless organizations and governments embrace advanced project leadership practices.

All is not lost. The good news is that there are many great examples of excellence in project management. Think of the iPhone, the 2014 World Cup-winning German team, the Airbus, the Panama Canal expansion, the Boeing 777, the Hong Kong–Zhuhai–Macao Bridge or the Renault–Nissan alliance.

What did these organizations and countries have in common? How did they successfully manage their projects? What lessons can we learn to ensure that, in the future, projects are significantly more successful, generate great wealth for the economy and impart benefits to our societies? Read on to discover the answers.

THE PROJECT CANVAS

INTRODUCING THE
PROJECT CANVAS.
WHAT REALLY MAKES
PROJECTS WORK?

Widely used management disciplines are often linked to a few simple frameworks that can be easily understood, and applied, not only by managers but also by the majority of individuals. Porter's Five Forces[63] and value chain[64] analysis help to make strategy a key area for every organization to apply. The Boston Consulting Group (BCG)'s Growth Share Product Portfolio matrix,[65] developed by BCG founder Bruce Henderson, helps us to understand product mix in a simple manner. And the seven Ps[66] in marketing, first proposed in 1960 by E. Jerome McCarthy (originally there were four Ps), are an essential framework to help us determine a product's or brand's market offering. These four frameworks are some of the best known and most widely used in their domains thanks to the ability of their founders to simplify complex matters.

In contrast, project management methods have tended to be too complex to be easily understood and applied by non-experts.

Stuart Crainer and Des Dearlove, founders of Thinkers50, the Oscars of management thinking according to the *Financial Times*, told me why project management has been ignored:

> People have an urge to overcomplicate and to reinvent. This is especially true in the realm of management thinking where ideas are perpetually relabelled and recycled. Project management sounds straightforward and somewhat traditional. A lot of managers are uncomfortable with these two things. They want something new and complicated, something that carries status. The reality that project management is complex, multifaceted, and universal seems to have passed people by. The fact that project management is not really taught at business schools perpetuates this.[67]

As outlined in chapter three, modern project management methods were developed primarily in the 1970s and 1980s by expert practitioners (at the beginning mostly engineers) for practitioners (also predominantly engineers). Their initial aim was to define standard project management processes and phases while also establishing common terms, roles, techniques and templates that could be used to plan and control any type of project, regardless of the area, size, complexity and industry.

The Project Management Institute (PMI)'s Project Management Body of Knowledge,[68] better known as the PMBOK®, is considered the global gold standard in project management. In the late 1980s, the PMI witnessed a need to put together all official documents and guides to improve the way projects were managed. First published by the PMI as a white paper in 1987, the PMBOK was an attempt to document and standardize accepted project management information and practices. The first edition was published in 1996 and became an essential tool in the project management profession, with over 2 million copies in circulation.

In 2017, the PMI launched the sixth edition of the PMBOK Guide, with a massive 756 pages (924 pages if we include the enclosed *Agile Practice Guide*). When compared with the fifth edition of the PMBOK, which was a meagre 589 pages, the sixth edition brings the largest content update since its creation. The *Agile Practice Guide* alone is 182 pages. In the sixth edition, the number of unique project-management-related tools and techniques proposed increased from 118 to 131.

Year	Edition	Pages	Knowledge Areas	Project Management Processes
1994	Exposure Draft	64	8	37
1996	First	176	9	37
2000	Second	211	9	39
2004	Third	390	9	44
2008	Fourth	467	9	42
2012	Fifth	589	9	47
2017	Sixth	756	9	49

FIGURE 4.

Exponential growth in the complexity of project management illustrated via the growth of the PMBOK

A 756-page book is a very rich and detailed document, with lots of technical information for the advanced project managers. However, it is obviously unlikely to be accessible for any leader or executive, let alone a normal person. It is very far from the simple yet insightful frameworks of the more mainstream disciplines referred to earlier.

The pivotal assumption of the project management methods has been that documenting every aspect of a project in detail will provide a high level of control of the planned activities during the implementation of the project. Many project managers ended up producing massive numbers of documents and swathes of paperwork, leading to an overall feeling that the role was primarily administrative. It has often been seen as low added value and distant from the frontline of the organization. The elements that matter most to executives – the rationale of the project, the business case and the delivery of the benefits to the organization – are often not a relevant part in the existing project management methodologies.

A final point about traditional project management techniques is that they work well when the context (internal and external) in which the project is implemented is stable and outcomes are predictable and fixed. However, they don't work well in the connected and fast-changing ecosystems that most organizations are operating in today.

Under these circumstances, it is not surprising that we saw the rise of agile, triggered by the Agile Manifesto,[69] written in February 2001 by 17 independent-minded software practitioners. They valued "individuals and interactions over processes and tools, working software over comprehensive documentation, customer collaboration over contract negotiation and responding to change over following a plan". This new methodology meant a reverse of some fundamental assumptions of project management in the changing environment driven by IT and the internet. It meant moving the focus from rigid, long-term and detailed planning to a flexible, short-term and iterative process. Agile removed most of the burdens that developers were facing working in a controlled and structured approach. The power shifted from the project manager to the IT developer. And this proved to be quite successful. Agile techniques were embraced, not only by the high-tech companies but also by almost every IT department in the world. As software itself is becoming a critical driver in almost all organizations, agile is now spreading to most aspects of work.[70] As I will explain in chapter eight when talking about agile organizations, these are all signs that the Project Revolution is here, and that it is here to stay.

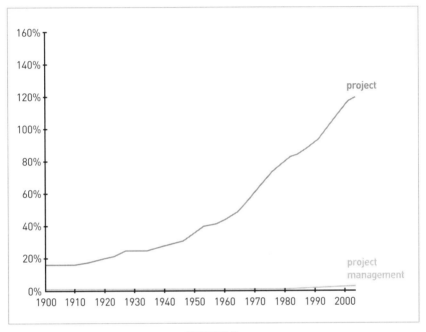

FIGURE 5.

The gap: evidence that project management is too complex to understand and be used by the non-expert

All in all, there is no doubt about the tremendous value of these collections of knowledge and best practices. Yet, as can be seen from **FIGURE 5**, which compares the numbers of occurrences of 'project' and 'project management' throughout the corpus of books accessed through Google Ngram Viewer, the disconnection between projects and project management is gigantic and continuing to grow. While the increase in projects has been spectacular – every country, region, organization and individual carries out numerous projects – the complexity just explained means that very few people use any form of project management method.

I always believed that there had to be a way to develop a simplified version of project management concepts and tools that would be easy to understand and to apply by any individual, business, official or organization, to any kind of project. This belief is reflected in the Project Canvas, a new framework that will reduce the gap between projects and project management and increase the adoption of best practices that will lead to more successful projects.

In my career of over 20 years as an executive educator, I have worked with hundreds of leaders who don't understand, or are not interested in, the day-to-day aspects of managing a project. The trouble is that the existing methodologies and courses are too complicated and train project managers to talk in technical terms about matters that don't interest the majority of stakeholders. Leaders, and those impacted by a project, primarily want to know the 'why' – the purpose, the benefits, the impact and the key elements that will make a project successful – and 'how' they can contribute to it.

Faced with the challenges of teaching project management to executives and MBAs, I developed the Project Canvas. If I wanted to keep them engaged and interested for days, I had to move away from the expert jargon – I had to simplify the language and the project management tools and techniques so that everyone was able to understand and apply them.

The framework is based on another premise. Every project – regardless of the industry, the organization (profit or non-profit), the sector (public or private), or whether it is personal or professional – is composed of exactly the same elements, which determine whether the project is a success or failure. If individuals, leaders and organizations focus on these elements and apply the techniques behind them, project success will almost be guaranteed.

In addition, as an expert practitioner, currently director of the Global Project Management Office at GlaxoSmithKline Vaccines and previously at BNP Paribas Fortis, I have a unique competitive advantage compared with other management experts from academia and/or the area of consulting: I am able to test in reality what works and what doesn't. And, not surprisingly, I have found that most of the standard project management theories are far from the reality. Like the saying goes: "In theory, theory and practice are the same. In practice, they are not."

The changes I propose are not intended to refute the methods of project management. On the contrary, my changes should make them more accessible. I want to universalize them. Neither I am against the agile methodology. I am a big fan of the improvements and shift in mindset it introduced. Instead, the Project Canvas leverages ideas from some of these concepts and allows anyone who is dealing with a project to apply them when needed.

The Project Canvas is composed of 14 dimensions – the ones that research has proven to influence and determine project success. These are grouped into four major domains. Each domain, or area of expertise, has a specific weight in the success of a project, which is indicated by a percentage. The four domains are:

- **Why**: the **rationale** and **expected benefits**, as well as the **purpose and passion** for launching and implementing the project successfully (**~20%**)
- **Who**: the **accountability** and the **governance** that will ensure the project is resourced and delivered (**~20%**)
- **What**, **How** & **When**: the **hard aspects** of projects (definition, design, plans, milestones, cost, risk, procurement) as well as the **soft** aspects (motivation, skills, stakeholders, change management, communication) (**~50%**)
- **Where**: the **organization**, the **culture**, the **priorities** and the **context** (internal and external) in which the project is being carried out (**~10%**).

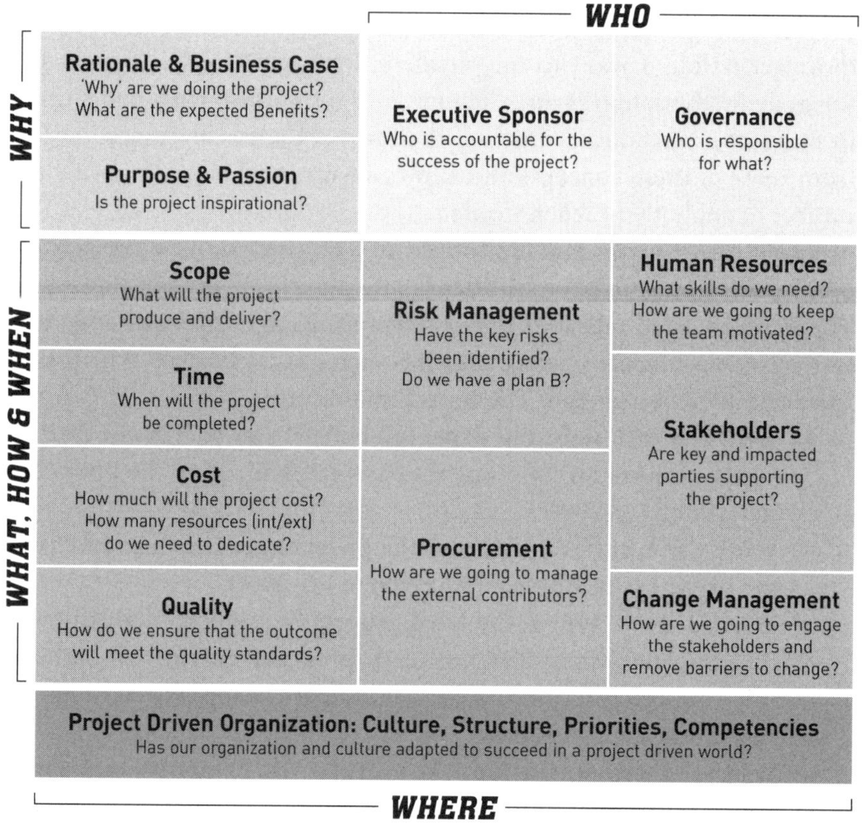

WHO

WHY

Rationale & Business Case
'Why' are we doing the project?
What are the expected Benefits?

Purpose & Passion
Is the project inspirational?

Executive Sponsor
Who is accountable for the
success of the project?

Governance
Who is responsible
for what?

WHAT, HOW & WHEN

Scope
What will the project
produce and deliver?

Time
When will the project
be completed?

Cost
How much will the project cost?
How many resources (int/ext)
do we need to dedicate?

Quality
How do we ensure that the outcome
will meet the quality standards?

Risk Management
Have the key risks
been identified?
Do we have a plan B?

Procurement
How are we going to manage
the external contributors?

Human Resources
What skills do we need?
How are we going to keep
the team motivated?

Stakeholders
Are key and impacted
parties supporting
the project?

Change Management
How are we going to engage
the stakeholders and
remove barriers to change?

Project Driven Organization: Culture, Structure, Priorities, Competencies
Has our organization and culture adapted to succeed in a project driven world?

WHERE

FIGURE 6.

The Project Canvas: four domains, 14 dimensions

In some projects, a domain might have more weight than others. However, as a project leader, owner or sponsor, you need to ensure that all four are addressed.

So, what makes the Project Canvas, this new project management framework, unique and different from all the other existing project management methods?

- It is made specifically for executives, officers and managers, but also for the newcomers to the profession: students, millennials, etc.
- It is simple and universal, and can be applied by anyone, in any kind of project.
- It focuses on value and benefits rather than processes and controls.
- It encourages the generation of benefits and impact faster.
- It ensures that every project has a purpose and aligns to the strategy of the organization.
- It focuses on implementation rather than detailed planning.
- It expands the horizons beyond the traditional project life cycle, looking at the pre-project and post-project phases.
- It is fast and flexible – it allows changes to the project whenever needed.
- It transforms project managers into true leaders of projects and organizations.
- It significantly increases the likelihood of project success.

The framework can be used by leaders and organizations at the beginning of a project to assess how well it has been defined and whether it is worth starting right away or needs further refinement. It can be applied to programmes, strategic initiatives and any other activities that can be considered projects.

The success of the Project Canvas lies on the following **12 principles**:

1. Developing a full business case is an arduous and lengthy process, yet projects need a clear rationale, purpose and connection to a higher strategy, before they are launched.
2. An active, ongoing and fully engaged executive sponsor is critical for project success.
3. Projects bring adjustments and changes to the status quo; thus resistance is expected and ought to be considered and addressed from the early stages.

4. Effective project managers have to be true leaders; they must understand the content and yet oversee the detailed activities to ensure successful completion.
5. People over processes: projects will always need motivated people to lead them, run them, execute them and close them.
6. Project failure is not always bad; often it is an opportunity to learn, to mature and to increase the focus on other more relevant projects.
7. Uncertainty is inherent in projects; risk management is essential to project management.
8. Change of initial project plans and requirements will most likely occur; agility is therefore indispensable throughout.
9. Project-driven organizations work across silos, allowing greater flexibility and faster response time to competition and changing market conditions than traditional hierarchical organizations.
10. Prioritization of projects is essential for increasing the success rate of project execution.
11. Project performance indicators should focus on outcomes (benefits, value creation, impact, opportunities and risks) instead of inputs (costs, time, material and scope).
12. Projects cannot go on forever; they have to be closed, even if sometimes not all tasks are fully completed.

Besides GlaxoSmithKline Vaccines and BNP Paribas Fortis, the Project Canvas has been implemented successfully in several organizations, yielding significant tangible improvements both in terms of return on investment and in terms of developing an execution-driven mindset and culture:

- a French–Dutch leading financial exchange company
- a leading Swiss biotech multinational
- a world top-ten cinema conglomerate with more than 100 theatres in Europe and North America
- a US-based top corporate law firm, one of the most prestigious in the world.

Let's now look into each of the four domains and their 14 dimensions. All of these elements appear, to a greater or lesser extent, in every project. Besides providing descriptions and real examples, I will include some recommended questions to ask in each dimension. The answers will lead to the most relevant information for the project. There are also sections about the tools to use. There are many available, but I have selected the ones that are the most straightforward, least complicated and easiest to apply, which are also the ones I use the most.

DOMAIN 1: WHY

The **Why** dimension covers the triggers and actual meaning of a project (the rationale and business case, and the purpose and passion), which will become the drivers once the project gets underway. The drivers are to obtain buy-in and resources (from the organization), to obtain attention and time from the executives, to obtain engagement from the members of the team and to obtain support from the individuals impacted by the project.

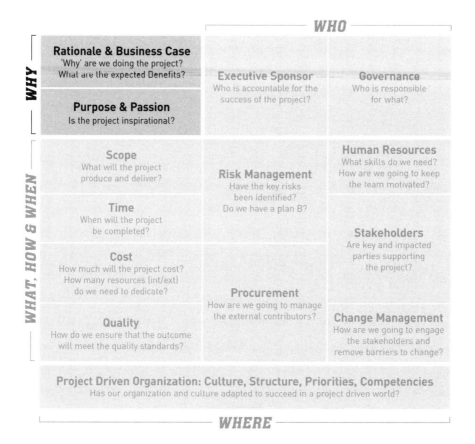

FIGURE 7.
Project Canvas – Domain 1: Why

RATIONALE AND BUSINESS CASE

All project management methodologies demand that projects always have a well-defined business case. Experience shows, however, that business cases have biases and subjective assumptions, especially concerning the financial benefits from the project, which often get inflated in order to make the project seem more attractive to the decision makers. Have you ever seen a project with a negative or meagre return being presented?

One of the best-known examples is Concorde, a British–French turbojet-powered supersonic passenger airliner that was operated from 1976 until 2003. The business case claimed there would be an enormous demand, estimating that up to 350 units would be sold.[71] Air France and British Airways were the only airlines to purchase and fly the Concorde. The company ultimately built 20 units and sold 14, at a loss of at least £4 billion.

There are hundreds of examples of overly optimistic predictions in high-profile projects. Another breakthrough project that has failed to deliver the expected benefits is the Energiewende energy project in Germany, which as described in chapter four is realizing limited benefits while costing German taxpayers an estimated €1.5 trillion by 2050. The issue with the Energiewende project is that the objectives (good practice) were overly optimistic and based on wrong assumptions (most probably to sell the project to the German people). Although there are some indications of good progress, the project as presented will still take a huge toll.

Don't get me wrong – preparation of a business case is a very useful exercise and should not be skipped or cut short. The thinking process, the research and the analysis of the options are helpful in getting a good understanding of the project and whether it is worth investing in or not. Nevertheless, I recommend caution regarding the business case and the projected returns (the financial figures), especially the expected benefits. Based on my experience, evaluating costs tends to be more accurate, to some extent, than evaluating benefits (there can be more unknowns, extra assumptions that extend over years, even decades).

My recommendation is to think in terms of the rationale for the project, to complement the business case.

In a very simple way, the two main rationales for launching a project are either to solve a problem or to capture an opportunity.

What is the problem we are going to solve with this project?

For example, the reconciliation project that began in the 1990s aimed to solve the problems in Rwanda caused by years of war between the Tutsi and Hutu peoples.

What is the opportunity we are going to capture with the project?

For example, the goal of the Boeing 777 project was to capture a huge opportunity in the commercial aerospace market. Airline customers wanted a wider fuselage cross-section, fully flexible interior configurations, short- to intercontinental-range capability, and an operating cost lower than existing models.

If you cannot answer either of these two questions easily and plainly, you should refrain from launching your project and research it further until you find the real rationale behind it.

Projects should have a clear rationale and at least one SMART objective (specific, measurable, action oriented, relevant and time-based; see further details below). Every project should have at least one clear and easy-to-memorize objective linked to the ultimate purpose. Business cases theoretically should have goal statements spelled out within them, yet practice tells us that these typically get diluted in endless swirls of information. Having one single objective for the project that uses the SMART technique is a necessity. It is incredible how many project managers talk about the products or deliverables of their project: the new software, the new platform, the expansion programme, the new company values, the reorganization, the digital transformation project … All of this is dull – it doesn't inspire either organizations or people to want to work on a project.

However, it is important to highlight that the project rationale and key objective should not be overly optimistic or based on the wrong assumptions. The project manager and sponsor have to ensure that the goals are realistic – or, even better, stretched but achievable.

- Does the project have a solid business case with a clear rationale?
- Does the project have a clear purpose with at least one quantifiable objective?

TOOLS TO USE

SMART objectives: The November 1981 issue of *Management Review* contained a paper by George T. Doran called "There's a S.M.A.R.T. Way to Write Management's Goals and Objectives."[72] Since then, SMART objectives have become an essential tool to focus people on what really matters and remove distractions. Every successful project needs at least one clearly articulated objective. SMART is an acronym for the following five elements:

- **S**pecific: provide the 'who' and the 'what' of the project.
- **M**easurable: focus on 'how much' the project will produce.
- **A**ction-oriented: trigger practical actions to achieve the project objective.
- **R**elevant: accurately address the purpose of the project.
- **T**ime-based: have a time frame indicating when the objective will be met.

An iconic example of a SMART objective is John F. Kennedy' moon landing project: he wanted the US to be the first country to put a man on the moon, before the end of the 1960s.

WHAT TO DO TO ENSURE PROJECT SUCCESS

Starting a project with an unclear rationale, an absent purpose and imprecise goals will most likely lead to project failure. Having clarity on the purpose and the benefits is not only important for making the decision on whether to invest or not; it also serves as key driver to engage and motivate the team members and the organization as a whole in supporting the project.

PURPOSE AND PASSION

Two of the newer elements in the Project Canvas are purpose and passion. Besides having a rationale, a project should be linked to a higher purpose. Jim Collins and Jerry Poras, authors of the business classic *Built to Last: Successful Habits of Visionary Companies,*[73] provided a useful definition of 'purpose', which we can adapt as follows:

> A project's purpose is its fundamental reason for being. An effective purpose reflects the importance people attach to the project's work – it taps their idealistic motivations – and gets at the deeper reasons for a project's existence beyond just making money.

Passion is a very strong feeling or an emotional connection about something or a strong belief in something. Passion is when you put more energy into something than is required to do it. It is more than just enthusiasm or excitement; passion is ambition that is materialized into actions intended to achieve something bigger. Passion is closely related to purpose. If passion and purpose are aligned, project success is almost guaranteed. Hunter S. Thompson, the gonzo journalist and novelist, once said: *"Anything that gets your blood racing is probably worth doing."*

People have enormous strengths; when a project they work on is connected to their purpose and passion, they can do amazing things, more than they have ever imagined. The best project leaders know that it is possible to tap into people's strengths through their hearts. The nice thing about it is that people don't have to be great at something to be passionate. Steve Jobs was not the world's greatest engineer, salesperson, designer or businessman. But he was uniquely good enough at all of these things, and was driven by his purpose and passion to do something far greater. Conversely, too, lack of conviction about a project can quickly be expanded to the rest of the team.

According to strategy implementation guru Jeroen De Flander, passion is the emotional connection that kick-starts travellers.[74] Successful strategists aim for the heart first.

- What is the emotional connection to the project?
- What would make people volunteer and contribute to the project?

Choosing the purpose: Defining your project's purpose is all about clarity and alignment. The purpose should not be fancy words – it has to be genuine and it has to feel meaningful. These are a few questions that can help you to determine the purpose of your project:
- Why does the project matter?
- What opportunity would be lost if the project were not carried out?
- To whom does the project matter most? The sponsor, the project leader, everyone?
- Why would anyone dedicate their precious time, energy and passion to the project?

Another easier method of finding the purpose of a project is to ask, "Why are you doing the project?" Usually it is necessary to ask this question five to seven times to get to the essence of the matter. Once you have the real reason, ask 'by when' and 'how much'. If after the exercise you don't reach something concrete, then I would strongly recommend that you do not start the project.

Questions to ask to identify a project's passion:
- Does the project have an emotional element?
- What makes the project great and unique?
- What will be remembered about the project ten years from now?
- What aspects would make people volunteer to participate and to contribute to the project?
- Is the project's passion aligned with the project's purpose?

Develop and share stories: As Jeroen De Flander explained to me: "Stories make messages stickier. Wrap a story around your message and it becomes 20 times easier for the listener to remember."[75] Stories put information in a context that people can relate to. Also, they offer a second benefit, which is to facilitate an emotional connection – "they reach for the heart". Finally, a good thing about stories, including project stories, is that they do not have to be invented, just spotted.

As Anders Inset, a world-leading business philosopher, once told me:

Bezos is not using PowerPoints, he's using storytelling, and people are tapping into that, getting an understanding of the topics, trying to visualize how to explain it. And that's how a project succeeds, and I'm a strong believer of that.[76]

WHAT TO DO TO ENSURE PROJECT SUCCESS

Psychologists have done extensive research on the impact positive thinking and 'believing in success' can have on individuals. In fact, success is a self-fulfilling prophecy. When we expect to succeed, we automatically mobilize our internal resources to achieve the expected, and all this happens without our rational consent. Moreover, when others believe in us, the dynamic is reinforced. That is why it is important for a project leader to create a positive environment where successes are applauded and the difficulties of a project are downplayed, so that a can-do spirit and attitude can be cultivated in the team. People need someone who believes in them so they can believe in themselves.

DOMAIN 2: WHO

The **Who** domain relates to the executive sponsor and governance, and it addresses the elements of accountability and allocation of responsibilities. An organization or business has a chief executive in charge and accountable for its operations. The same should happen with a project, in the role of the executive sponsor, who is the ultimate accountable person. Yet, more often than not, the role is either not understood or not performed consistently with the importance it has for the success of the project. Establishing a clear governance structure at the beginning of the initiative is essential too.

FIGURE 8.

Project Canvas – Domain 2: Who

EXECUTIVE SPONSOR

Many projects start without it being decided who is ultimately accountable for their successful delivery. As projects tend to go across departments, business units and countries, they are often prone to 'shared accountability and collective sponsorship.' As a result, many executives feel responsible, yet no one is really accountable for driving the project to completion.

In many projects, the selection of the executive sponsor is not done purposefully. The role is often seen as something symbolic, often a reflection of authority: "The more projects I sponsor, the more powerful I am." This is one of the most common errors that lead to systematic project failure.

Organizations need to understand that the executive sponsor is one of the most vital and influential roles in any project, especially those that are strategic and transversal. The more complex the project, the more critical the executive sponsor role and the more time it demands.

Once, when I was speaking to the CEO of a large global telecoms company, he bluntly admitted that, "Currently, I am the executive sponsor of 18 projects. The five projects that I dedicate time to follow through – where I support the project leader and team, and chair the steering committee – go much better than the 13 that I sponsor but don't dedicate any time to."

Let's look at an example of executive sponsorship. On 6 August 2007, over 90% of votes at Fortis's shareholder meetings in Brussels and Utrecht backed one of Europe's largest takeovers ever in the financial industry. The €71 billion (mostly cash) offer by Fortis, Royal Bank of Scotland and Spain's Banco Santander was made for the Netherlands' largest bank, ABN AMRO. On 3 October 2008, Fortis Bank was broken up after experiencing extreme difficulty financing its part of the joint acquisition of ABN AMRO. After receiving a bailout from the Benelux governments, its Belgian banking operations were disposed of in a fire-sale to BNP Paribas, after its insurance and banking subsidiaries in the Netherlands had been nationalized by the Dutch government and renamed back to ABN AMRO.

Over the period of 14 months that the project lasted before it collapsed, the ultimate executive sponsor, Fortis's CEO, Jean-Paul Votron, was seen in Amsterdam on only two occasions. Splitting and integrating the acquired ABN AMRO bank was a tremendous challenge that generated a high level of resistance and required a fast decision-making process. The absence of Fortis's CEO was seen by the old ABN AMRO directors and employees as a sign of weakness, which they exploited by not supporting the separation project and avoiding sharing vital information – such as customer data – needed to advance the project according to the tight deadlines. Critical decisions (such as management appointments) needed to be made quickly but ended up taking weeks and sometimes months. In the end, the lack of executive support for the most important strategic initiative of the bank became one of the main reasons for the failure and the destruction of more than €20 billion of shareholders' value.

KEY QUESTIONS TO ASK
- Has the executive sponsor been appointed?
- Are they ready to dedicate enough time (for a strategic project, between 20% and 40% of their time, depending on the project phase) to drive the project to success?

TOOLS TO USE
Checklist: How to select the right executive sponsor

Most of the time, the executive sponsor is naturally selected, based on where the project originates. However, here are a few criteria that may help you to choose the right person:
- has the highest vested interest in the outcome of the project
- owner of a budget, both financial and resources
- high enough up in the organization to be able to make budget decisions
- ready to dedicate at least one day of their time each week to support the project
- preferably has a good understanding of the technical matters of the project.

Checklist: Responsibilities of the executive sponsor
- ensure the project's strategic significance
- establish approval and funding for the project
- promote support from key stakeholders
- resolve conflicts and make decisions
- be accessible and approachable – on-call support for the project leader
- participate in periodic reviews
- chair the steering committee
- encourage recognition
- support closure review
- be ultimately accountable for the project.

The *Harvard Business Review* article "How to Be an Effective Executive Sponsor" provides good insights on the expectations for the role.[77]

WHAT TO DO TO ENSURE PROJECT SUCCESS
Appoint the most appropriate executive sponsor – one person, not many. They will be accountable for the outcome of the project; it should become a priority for them.

GOVERNANCE

The executive sponsor, together with the project manager, should define the project governance. The governance in a project is represented by a project chart in which the various contributing roles and decision-making bodies are defined.

One of the most important bodies in a project is the steering committee, which is chaired by the executive sponsor and run by the project manager. The members and the frequency with which they meet often determine the importance the project has for the organization. I remember being on a large integration project of two European banks. Its steering committee, chaired by the CEO, met every day at 5pm to discuss the status of the merger. Imagine the pressure that this reflected on the organization. For all of us, it was evident that the integration project was the number-one priority, and we had to show progress every day. In contrast, I have also worked on a project where the steering committee met every three months. In addition, most senior leaders didn't show up because they had other priorities, and those who were present hardly remembered what the project was about. The first project was extremely successful, the second a complete failure.

The second element in the governance is the project's core team. This is the group of individuals (and their teams) that will dedicate the most time in designing, planning and developing the solutions and outcomes of the projects. Each of the contributing parties should have a member in the core team, including key vendors (consultants and subcontractors). The project manager is in charge of coordinating and supervising the core team activities and progress. It is recommended to have a core team meeting once per week, increasing the frequency when the project struggles or is closer to a key milestone.

Three of the organizational challenges faced by projects that executives need to be aware of and that strong governance will address are:

- **Resources are often not fully dedicated to the project and have other responsibilities:** For example, a Java development expert whose main job is to keep the website up and running is asked to join a digitalization project. Her current responsibilities are not modified, therefore her contribution to the strategic project will be on top of her day-to-day job. Not being fully dedicated will have an impact on the speed of the project.
- **Resources have different reporting lines outside the project:** For example, a legal expert is part of a GDPR (General Data Protection Regulation) project, which is led by the vice president of the business. The legal expert is not participating in the weekly project team meetings. The vice president has tried to convince the legal expert to join, but as she doesn't report to him she doesn't feel obliged to follow his instructions.
- **Departments' objectives are different and regularly more important than the project's objectives:** For example, a finance controller is required to participate in the development of the business case of a large company-wide project. However, his direct boss, the CFO, is under pressure to finalize the annual accounts,

a key objective for the finance department. Despite having some tight deadlines, the project is at the mercy of the CFO's willingness to cooperate.

Without strong governance, the inertia of the organization will make a project battle for resources and attention, leading the project to delays and eventually failure.

To address these organizational forces, senior leaders need to play a key role in supporting the project and providing the resources and time required to complete the work. Therefore, it is essential for the success of large transversal projects that senior leaders assume the steering committee role and responsibilities reflected in the organizational chart, which also should reflect the core team and the different contributors in the project.

KEY QUESTIONS TO ASK

- Has the project's steering committee been established, including the frequency with which it will meet?
- Has the project core team been established, including the frequency with which it will meet?
- Are appointed and selected members committed to participate and contribute to the success of the project?

TOOLS TO USE

Checklist: Best practices for establishing and running a steering committee

- Does the project require major investments and impact large segments (or the entirety) of the organization, region or country?
- Have you identified which resources, departments, suppliers, partners, etc. need to contribute to the project? If any of them has an involvement of 10% or more of the total budget, they should be part of the steering committee.
- Are the members of the steering committee budget owners (of resources, capital, etc.) with enough decision-making power?
- How much momentum and pressure does the project need? The higher this is, the more frequently the steering committee should meet.

Use the Responsibility Assignment Matrix (RACI)[78] to reflect who does what: This is a simple tool used to cross-match key activities with the various roles in a project and core team. It considers who should be:

- responsible: for carrying out the activity
- accountable: the ultimate owner of the activity
- consulted: individuals or groups that need to be consulted and provide input
- informed: individuals or groups that ought to be informed.

WHAT TO DO TO ENSURE PROJECT SUCCESS

Define and agree on a strong governance structure to ensure the commitment of the organization. Establish clear roles and responsibilities. Make sure that all contributors and the core team know the role they play and how much time and resources are requested from their teams.

Finally, appoint the right level in the hierarchy of decision makers – senior roles, often budgets owners – to the steering committee, and determine the frequency of their meetings. A steering committee should meet at least once a month. For a strategic project, a steering committee meeting every two weeks will create momentum. The higher the frequency, the higher the pressure.

DOMAIN 3: WHAT, HOW & WHEN

The **What**, **How** & **When** domain covers the fundamental elements that constitute the project. They can be split into technical areas and people-related elements. These are the project fundamentals: hard aspects (definition, design, plans, milestones, cost, risk and procurement) and soft aspects (motivation, skills, stakeholders, change and communication). Addressing all of the elements at the right time and with enough depth will increase the chances of project success. As opposed to the other three domains, which have to be tackled from the senior level of the organization, the fundamental areas in this domain are the responsibility of the project leader.

FIGURE 9.
Project Canvas – Domain 3: What, How & When

SCOPE

Understanding and agreeing what the project will consist of and deliver – the scope – is one of the *raisons d'être* of project management. Other terms for scope include specifications, detailed requirements, design and functionality. The scope is the most important element in making an accurate estimation of the cost, duration, plan and benefits of the project. Various tools can be used to try to determine what the outcome of the project will look like, yet this remains one of the most difficult tasks.

Depending on the type of project, there is a good chance that it will be possible, more or less, to clearly define the scope in the early stages of the project (e.g. a property development initiative). There are other projects, however, in which the scope will be impossible to determine with precision at the beginning (e.g. a digital transformation initiative). Therefore, duration and costs estimated at the beginning of the project will mostly be wrong. Basically, if the project has a vague scope, the time and cost estimated will be utterly wrong.

The other common challenge is that even if the scope has been well defined at the beginning of the project, there is a good chance that it will change during the lifecycle of the project (also known as 'scope creep'). This will again impact the duration, cost, plans and benefits of the project. The more the scope changes (i.e. in terms of design, requirements, functionality, features and characteristics), the more challenging it is to deliver the project successfully and according to the initial plan.

KEY QUESTIONS TO ASK

- Has the scope been clearly defined? Do you know, with precision, how the outcome of the project should look? From 0% to 100%, how certain are you that the scope will not change?
- Is there a clear process for managing changes to the scope?

TOOLS TO USE

BOSCARD Framework: Created in the 1980s by Cap Gemini to help define scope of projects, this framework consists of the following seven questions:

1. **Background – what is the background of the project?** Describe the relevant facts to show an understanding of the environmental, political, business and other contexts in which the project will be carried out.
2. **Objective – what are the key objectives?** State the goals of the project and demonstrate an understanding of its business rationale (the 'why').
3. **Scope – what is the solution the project will implement?** Describe what the project will develop and break its various stages down into milestones. Describe the resources that will be made available and the corresponding external partners, if applicable.
4. **Constraints – what are the key constraints to delivering the project successfully?** Describe the key challenges and blocking factors to be addressed in planning the project.
5. **Assumptions – what are the main assumptions taken?** State the key hypothesis that has been used to define the project rationale, objectives, plan and budget. If assumptions change later, it might justify a renegotiation of the project.
6. **Risks – what are the risks that could make the project fail?** List the risks that may materialize and affect the realization of the objectives of the project. Also, list any risks that could have an impact on the timeline and finances (such as tax and other transaction costs).
7. **Deliverables – what are the desired outcomes of the project?** Describe the key elements that will be produced by the project, and how they connect to each other and to the project objectives.

By addressing each area, you can be clear on what is expected to be done and not done, and have an upfront discussion on the boundaries of the project with the executive sponsor and key stakeholders.

WHAT TO DO TO ENSURE PROJECT SUCCESS

At the beginning of the project, gather the main stakeholders and key contributors together to define and agree to the scope, in as detailed a manner as possible. Don't be afraid of taking some extra days to address major uncertainties. A delay of one week during the scoping phase can save significant time. If the uncertainty leads to a change during the implementation, it will probably lead to a longer delay, and perhaps derail the whole project altogether.

TIME

"Time is money": this famous phrase, attributed to Benjamin Franklin, is an absolute in projects. Time is one of the major characteristics of projects in that, unless there is an articulated, compelling, official and publicly announced deadline, there is a good chance that the project will be delivered later than originally planned. Delays in projects mean, besides extra costs, a loss of benefits and expected revenues, both having a tremendous negative impact on the business case of the initiative. A project without a deadline should not be considered a project – better call it an experiment, an exploration or daily business activities.

Olympic Games, World Cups and World Expositions are massive projects that have fixed deadlines, announced and established years in advance. The way these projects are implemented varies significantly according to the means and the country's working culture: some are finished in advance (e.g. London 2012), others just in time (Rio de Janeiro 2016). However, what is fantastic is that, despite all the challenges and different ways of dealing with projects, the Olympic Games are always delivered on time!

As we will see later, another problem in projects is that the people working on them most often have other jobs and duties that will take most of their attention. They are hardly ever 100% dedicated to the project. Time, and deadlines, are essential to help people to focus and to exert some pressure on getting the work done.

A great example of the immense power of deadlines is the project of landing the first man on the moon. When he announced his bold dream, in May 1961, US president John F. Kennedy set a clear deadline for it: "by the end of the 1960s". That deadline stuck in people's minds, and it pushed them to work together to achieve an impossible dream. That deadline was one of the project's biggest success factors. Without that deadline, it is uncertain that humans would yet have landed on the moon. The bill for the 1969 moon landing by the Apollo 11 Lunar Module came to $25.4 billion;[79] it remains one of the most expensive projects in history yet one of humanity's greatest accomplishments.

Time in projects is peculiar. The week at the beginning of a project is the same as a week at the end of the project, but it doesn't feel the same. Closer to the deadline, people will become nervous and tend to make mistakes. The role of the project leader is therefore similar to the role of the conductor of an orchestra. They set the tempo and intermediary deadlines, which vary throughout the project life cycle.

One of the most significant issues with the failed Google Glass project was that Google was not able to build momentum around it; the company didn't set a definite date for the official launch of the product. Consumers were informed neither about an actual product release date nor where they could purchase the product. In fact, Google co-founder Sergey Brin suggested that Glass should be treated like a finished product when Google started selling it to the public, despite everyone in the lab knowing it was more of a prototype with significant twists to be worked out. Google should have learned from Apple on how to create buzz about new products with a public release date.

KEY QUESTIONS TO ASK

- Does the project have a clear deadline well known by everyone, including external stakeholders?
- Is the deadline realistic and likely to be achieved?

TOOLS TO USE

Top-down, bottom-up planning: The best and most accurate way to create a plan and establish a realistic deadline is by first having an initial high-level orientation on the best timing to complete the project (e.g. launch date or opening day). After breaking down the project into activities, perform a bottom-up plan and assess whether the initial deadline is realistic to achieve. If not, think of ways to reduce the duration of the project: for example, by adding resources, by working in parallel or by doing the project in different phases. When possible, and to increase the pressure on the team, reduce the deadline by 5% to 20%. Also, to maintain the momentum, it is important to work with intermediary deadlines (or milestones) of about three to six weeks. With anything beyond that, there is a risk that people will drag along and procrastinate until they are close to the milestone date and then rush, with the risk of impacting the final quality.

WHAT TO DO TO ENSURE PROJECT SUCCESS

It is essential that every project has a clear deadline. For the most relevant and strategic ones, the executive team has to commit to it, and it has to be officially announced. That way people will keep the end date of the project in their minds, all the time, creating the necessary focus that will help them when they have to decide how to allocate their time. A clear deadline will create pressure to make the project a success.

COST

Budget in projects is composed mostly of the time dedicated by the project resources. These mainly include the people working on the project plus all other investments (consultants, material, software, hardware, etc.) required to develop the scope of the project. Budget is, together with time and scope, the third main constraint in traditional project management. Without budget, there is no project.

As explained earlier, the accuracy of the budget estimates depends on the scope's definition and its stability.

In the yearly budgeting and resource allocation cycle, organizations usually have two main types of budgets: capital and operational. The capital expenditure (often called CAPEX) budget is fully allocated to large investment projects, which makes the execution of projects easier. The operational expenditure (often called OPEX) budget is often higher, used for the resources that are running the organization. Two of the most frequently encountered challenges for organizations are the ambiguity that arises in projects that are funded from the OPEX budget, and the allocation of resources between operations and project activities.

Dedicating sufficient resources to a project is critical for ensuring its success.

Some projects have the luxury of receiving an unlimited budget. This helps to engage more resources, accelerate the project and deliver it successfully. This is often the case for projects that are launched and supported by senior leaders or top officials. It was true for some of the majestic projects built in the Middle East in the past decade – for example, the Burj Khalifa, at 828 metres the tallest building in the world, was sponsored by the sheikh of Dubai. The project didn't have any problems with budget. Construction began in 2004, with the exterior completed five years later and the building opened to the public in 2010.

However, having an unlimited budget is not a guarantee of success. If some of the key elements described in this section are missing, there are chances that the project will fail. A clear example is the launch of the Obama administration's Healthcare.gov website project. When the website was launched on 1 October 2013, it collapsed, causing tremendous reputational damage. Yet budget was not a constraint.

KEY QUESTIONS TO ASK
- Does the project have a fully dedicated budget that has been well estimated?
- Could the project's budget absorb overruns?

TOOLS TO USE
Top-down, bottom-up budget estimation: It is important to note that most of the cost in a project is the time spent by the team members (human resources) to perform the project activities. The best and most accurate way to create a budget is by first having an initial high-level (**top-down**) orientation on the total project cost. Identify the potential budget available and look at the costs of similar past projects. Then, after breaking the project down into activities, estimate the cost of each activity (**bottom up**).

As with the planning, this exercise should be carried out together with the main contributors to the project. Some activities will be performed by external parties; they have to provide their cost projections. Some activities or extra cost could transpire after the project has been completed. Adding together the costs of all the activities will provide an accurate view of the total investment required to carry out the project. Large projects usually include a contingency amount (5–10%) of the total estimated cost to handle unforeseen expenses. Compare the bottom-up estimate with the initial top-down estimate and see whether there is a big gap. If that is the case, and there is an important budget constraint, consider reducing the scope or even re-evaluating carrying out the project.

WHAT TO DO TO ENSURE PROJECT SUCCESS

The budget is derived directly from the scope of the project and the urgency to deliver. The more detailed the scope and the more fixed it is, the better the budget will be estimated. To reduce the risk of budget overruns, never allocate the total amount of the budget to the project at the beginning. Break it down into portions. Establish quarterly review cycles to check status and budget consumption. If the project's original business case is still valid, release another portion of budget. If the project is having serious problems, ignore sunk costs and consider seriously cancelling it.

QUALITY

Ensuring that the outcome of the project meets the quality expectations is an integral part of project management, yet it is often overlooked or not a priority. Often teams focus on doing the work and leave the quality part to the end of the project, when adjustments are most expensive.

It is the responsibility of the project manager to ensure that a project meets, or exceeds, the expected quality. Lack of quality should lead to the cancellation of the project.

Some projects require official and significant quality validation tests in order to start commercial production. This is the case with many infrastructure, production, life science and engineering projects.

For IT development, it is common to do user testing and other simulations to ensure that the end product satisfies the needs of the organization. Traditionally, the testing of new systems was done towards the end of the project, often leading to additional work and delays in the schedule. Nowadays, with agile development methods, quality checks are done almost on a weekly basis.

One of Apple's greatest strengths is that it makes its products look and feel easy to use. But there was nothing easy about making the iPhone – its inventors say the process was often nerve-wracking. Steve Jobs wanted to see a demo of everything. Designers would often create mock-ups of a single design element – such as a button on the iPhone – up to 50 times until it met his stellar quality standards.[80]

KEY QUESTIONS TO ASK

- Have the expected quality and acceptance criteria of the project been defined?
- Does the project include periodic quality checks, including end customer and stakeholders' feedback?

TOOLS TO USE

Quality assurance and quality control: Achieving success in a project requires both quality assurance (QA) and quality control (QC). Although QA and QC are closely related concepts, they are distinct. QC is used to verify the quality of the outputs of the project,[81] while QA is the process of managing for quality.[82]

In simple terms, make sure your project has a process or method to test whatever the project is delivering (whether a product, system, bridge, phone, plane or something else) and that the project plan includes regular quality checks, prototyping and testing time.

WHAT TO DO TO ENSURE PROJECT SUCCESS

Quality has to be embedded in the life of the project. Involve the quality experts – internal and/or external – and ensure they commit time to your project. Quality checks, prototyping, testing, rehearsals and so on all have to be incorporated into the project plan and reported upon. The sooner potential deviations and faults in the end product are found, the less impact they will have in the project's progress, budget and timelines.

RISK MANAGEMENT

Risk management is one of the most important techniques in project management and an essential duty of the project manager. Bluntly, if a project fails, it is because the risks that caused the failure were either not identified or not mitigated on time by the project team.

The pure nature of projects, which is to produce something new and unique, is intrinsically uncertain. Therefore, one of the central purposes of project management is to manage the risk of the project. If a project is being carried out for the first time, superior attention to risks is needed.

Monte Carlo simulation, or probability simulation, is an advanced technique used to understand the effect of risk and uncertainty in large projects, based on what-if-scenarios. It was invented by a Polish atomic nuclear scientist named Stanislaw Ulam[83] in 1940 and named after the city in Monaco famed for its casinos and games of chance. The formula provides a series of possible values for each risk to help decision making and planning.

The Monte Carlo simulation method has many benefits: it helps in evaluating the risk of a project, predicting the chances of failure, and building a realistic project budget and schedule. It is still very much in use today in large infrastructure and capital projects.

As shown in FIGURE 10, the sooner the risks are identified and (if necessary) mitigated, the less costly it will be for the project. A great example of this phenomenon of late risk identification is the French railway operator SNCF, which in 2014 ordered 2,000 new trains that were too big for many of the stations they needed to visit.[84] The train operator admitted failing to verify measurements before ordering its new stock. As a result of the mistake, some 1,300 platforms had to be modified at a cost of €50 million.

One assessment that is often ignored is the additional risk that a project brings to an organization. Adding an extra project to an organization that is already running too many projects will increase the risk of failure. There have been several cases of bankruptcy triggered by a company launching too many projects. The collapse of Fortis Bank is one of the most notorious.

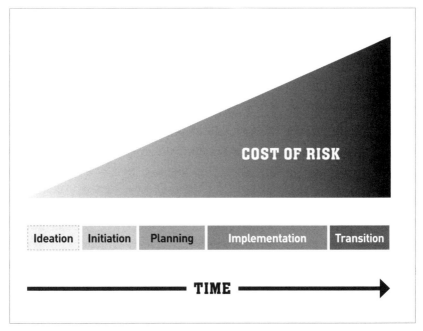

FIGURE 10.
Cost of risk – the later the impact, the higher the cost

EXAMPLE

Risk management is also about having a plan B. What if at D-Day one of the risks impacts the project, or what if something unforeseen happens just before launch? A typical example is an outdoor event: what is the alternative if it rains?

It is well known that, during the launch of the first iPhone, the new gadget was not fully ready. Yet, the demo in January 2007 at the Apple Convention looked seamless to the audience. The project team at Apple were aware of the risks with the iPhone and mitigated them through detailed risk management. They designed a plan to use several iPhones, one for each key feature (e.g. making a call, surfing the internet) throughout the demo. The team rehearsed several times to ensure that there were no last-minute surprises. Despite the challenges, thanks to the detailed risk management, they were able to successfully introduce the iPhone.

KEY QUESTIONS TO ASK
- How risky is the project and can the organization cope with it?
- Have major risks that could severely impact the project been identified and mitigated?

TOOLS TO USE

Risk matrix: The risk matrix is the most commonly used tool for assessing the risks that might impact a project. Perform a brainstorming session with the key project stakeholders to identify risks that could impact, or even terminate, the project. Define the importance of each risk by considering the probability or likelihood of the risk occurring and the severity of the impact. This is not a scientific approach, rather a simple mechanism to increase visibility and control of the major risks and take mitigating actions whenever management of the project feels it is appropriate.

FIGURE 11 is an example of a risk matrix that you can use as a basis to identify and manage the risks in your project. For each risk, identify where it falls on the grid.

IMPACT

PROBABILITY	Trivial	Minor	Moderate	Mayor	Severe
Almost Certain	Medium	High	High	Extreme	Extreme
Likely	Medium	Medium	High	High	Extreme
Possible	Low	Medium	Medium	High	Extreme
Unlikely	Low	Medium	Medium	Medium	High
Rare	Low	Low	Medium	Medium	High

FIGURE 11.
Project risk assessment matrix

WHAT TO DO TO ENSURE PROJECT SUCCESS

Involve experts, stakeholders and past project team members in early discussions to identify the key risks of the project. Also, assess the risks for the organization of not doing the project. And don't forget to gauge the additional risk that the organization will bear by investing in the project.

Some projects will have thousands of risks, so you don't want to make the risk management process too bureaucratic. Even if it is important to start broadly with the identification of risks, the focus should be on the most likely and most severe risks.

PROCUREMENT

Most people think that procurement has nothing to do with projects and project management. Yet, it is one of the main reasons why so many projects fail. In the case of the activities needed to run an organization, the employees have the knowledge and experience required to perform the activities efficiently and effectively. By contrast, projects tend to have a novelty component; therefore, the need to hire external capabilities to deliver the project is much higher. Consulting companies provide advice and resources to organizations carrying out projects. As projects are temporary assignments, it is cheaper to engage external capacity during the project than to hire internal resources. Important projects, such as mergers and acquisitions, require significant involvement of consultants and third parties, often reaching up to 30–40% of the total resources in the acquisition project.

In the public sector, the importance of procurement is well known. Projects carried out by governments rely fully on external resources, contractors, consultants, experts and so on, reaching close to 100% of the resources dedicated to the project. Projects frequently take the form of public–private partnerships, which entail a collaborative approach to executing public sector projects. Therefore, public organizations need very advanced procurement practices. From the selection process to the execution of the project, public procurement plays an instrumental role. The challenges of procurement in the public sector include a heavy burden of procedures that need to be applied (affecting agility) and low fees (which tend to lead to less experienced consultants being hired).

EXAMPLE

The public sector often struggles with large-scale projects. Many administrations simply lack the experts to manage complex construction projects. The Elbphilharmonie Hamburg reached a level of complexity that was apparently too much for the state to handle. In 2007, the construction was scheduled to be finished by 2010 with an estimated cost of €77 million. Construction work officially ended on 31 October 2016 at a cost of €789 million.

Slimmed-down administrations are barely capable of efficiently controlling construction projects, and supervisory boards staffed according to the proportions of power held by political parties fail when it comes to monitoring projects. Power and decision-making end up in the hands of the vendors of the project, who are able to draw significantly more benefits than what was initially planned, at the cost of public funds.

KEY QUESTIONS TO ASK

- How many subcontractors does the project have?
- Do the project organization chart and roles and responsibilities include the key vendors?
- Do the vendors have incentives and penalties in place to deliver the project successfully?

TOOLS TO USE

Procurement management process: Procuring goods and services from external suppliers is critical in many projects. Their performance can reflect on the performance of the overall project. It is therefore crucial to establish a procurement management process to help administer the purchases of services and products from external suppliers needed to carry out the project. The process will enable:

- identifying the best suppliers
- negotiating the best terms

- reviewing supplier performance
- identifying and resolving supplier performance issues
- communicating the status to the project steering committee.

WHAT TO DO TO ENSURE PROJECT SUCCESS

Failing to coordinate external resources can lead to project failure, especially in the public sector, which heavily relies on vendors, consultants and contractors. Failed IT projects, such as the Healthcare. gov example (see the section above on cost), often result from poor management of external resources. The larger the amount or the higher the dependency on external resources, the more attention the project manager needs to pay to procurement. It is not an area that they should excel at, but it does require a good initial assessment of needs, effective vendor selection and constant monitoring throughout the lifecycle of the project.

The number of subcontractors should be determined by the specific competencies needed to deliver the project. In some instances, there will be several hundred, but the key is to ensure that they feel part of the team and are overseen by the project team.

It is essential to define clear roles and responsibilities and ensure that the project leadership remains within the organization. It is also recommended to find ways to incentivize external parties to stay committed and engaged to deliver according to the specifications of the project within budget.

HUMAN RESOURCES

Today, project managers need to be project leaders too, especially for the more complex and cross-functional projects. These require pulling resources across the organization and changing the old status quo. In fact, we can argue that the best project managers are leaders but also entrepreneurs – they are the CEOs of their projects.

Marshall Goldsmith, the world's number-one executive coach, told me:

Executives tend to see project managers as technical experts: very tactical people, focused on the detail challenges of the project. Modern leadership is moving into facilitation. The best CEO's I have coached are great facilitators. Therefore, the project managers of the future will have to become project leaders, strong in facilitation, rather than technical experts.[85]

Over the past decades, we have seen the focus shifting from the original areas of project management, also known as hard skills (scope, planning, scheduling and estimation), to soft skills (leadership, stakeholder management and communication). A good project manager can navigate the organization, motivate the team, sell the project's benefits to the key stakeholders, and deliver on scope, on time and within budget. Other skills required by successful project manager are:

- understanding the strategic and business aspects of the project
- influencing and persuading stakeholders at all levels
- leading in a matrix organization
- creating a high-performing team from a group of individuals
- providing feedback and motivating the project team
- monitoring the progress of the project work.

Unfortunately, good project managers are scarce. And, because companies have many strategic projects, such projects are often led by managers who do not have all of the necessary qualifications.

Selecting the right project manager with the right skills and experience is a critical success factor. Yet, many organizations don't reflect too much on this step, or the process is not transparent. Another recurrent issue is that very often projects are seen as a development opportunity for high-potential managers. They take the lead of a large strategic project for two years to get exposure with top management. At the same time, they build complementary skills not required in a line function. The problem is that they don't see projects as a long-term career, thus they are not interested in learning about project management in more depth. So, they struggle as they are not aware of the tools and techniques that will make the project a success.

Another aspect to consider is project staffing. Projects need people to be carried out. Ensuring that the organization has available resources, with the right skills, expertise and experience to implement the project, is an essential responsibility of senior management. Yet, it is surprising to see how many organizations launch projects without doing a capacity check prior to confirming the initiative.

If the right resources and competencies are not available within the organization, they can either be developed through training or acquired externally. Often, the best and most experienced staff (e.g. developers) are booked on other tasks and projects. If their contribution is not suitably planned, the project is going to suffer. Lack of availability of required resources leads to delays and frequently to project failure.

Besides availability, a key aspect of project success is team commitment. As mentioned earlier, project resources tend to have other responsibilities besides their contribution to the project. Commitment to the project is never a given, especially because employees are often asked to join in such a way that it is difficult for them to refuse (we've all received an email that asks us to 'kindly' agree to something but where in reality we don't have much choice). They are ready to contribute, often for free and/or giving up some of their private time, only because they want to be part of an amazing experience.

Often project managers are asked to complete extensive and often time-consuming reports to inform senior management about the progress of a project. **Yet, a quick and easy way to assess the health of a project is by asking the project manager two questions:**
1. **How much time do you dedicate to this project?**
2. **How committed are you to the project?**

Ideally, the answer to both should be 100%, which increases the chances of success. However, often project managers are not fully dedicated to one single project. Depending on the project, 50% is still acceptable, but below that will increase the risk of failure due to potentially feeble oversight and weak management.

"We're starting a new project. It's so secret, I can't even tell you what the new project is. I cannot tell you who you will work for. What I can tell you is that if you choose to accept this role, you're going to work harder than you ever have in your entire life. You're going to have to give up nights and weekends probably for a couple of years as we make this product"[86] – so Scott Forstall, head of the iPhone software division, might have explained to his potential team members.

The project team was one of the most talented groups of individuals in recent history. The best engineers, the best programmers and the best designers were selected to join the team.[87] And not part time, one or half a day a week, which is most companies' standard approach with their strategic projects. The chosen people were fully discharged from all their duties and were assigned full time to the project effective immediately. Project Purple became their life.

Forstall later explained that Steve Jobs had told him he could have anyone in the company on his team. And the high quality of the team didn't stop with the technians. Jobs decided to include the best leadership team too, starting with Jonny Ive, the designer of the iPod and MacBook, who was put in charge of the look of the handset.

KEY QUESTIONS TO ASK

- Has a professional project manager being appointed to lead the project?
- Does the organization have sufficient capacity and the required skills to run the project successfully?

TOOLS TO USE

Ask the project leader two questions to help assess whether the project is in good hands:

- **How much of your time do you dedicate to this project?** Strategic projects require 100% dedication. Anything below that can lead to distraction and to a reduction in the pressure on the project. Often project managers are asked to lead several projects simultaneously. In my experience, it is hard to lead more than three important projects at the same time, and it is also hard to manage an important project while having a full-time position in the day-to-day activities of the organization.

- **How committed are you to the success of the project?** Knowing that the project will face challenges, if the project manager and resources are not committed, the project will most likely be a total failure. A great example of this positive thinking is Alan Mulally, the project manager in charge of building the Boeing 777, a massive undertaking, in the worst circumstances, after the terrorist attacks of 11 September 2001 and with Boeing struggling to survive. Yet, his strong commitment and full-time dedication drove a project of 10,000 team members to create one of the most advanced aircraft in the world.

Lack of conviction in a project can quickly spread to the rest of the team. When the conviction and morale drops significantly, the sponsor should intervene and find ways to restore confidence, either by taking corrective actions or, eventually, by replacing the project manager.

WHAT TO DO TO ENSURE PROJECT SUCCESS

At the beginning of a project, senior management needs to assess and confirm the resources capacity and availability to work on the project. They need to ensure the resources and the skills required to develop the solution are there. It is necessary to anticipate potential bottlenecks by freeing up resources or engaging external capacity and expertise.

Establish a standard process to appoint the best-prepared project manager to lead the project. They should have technical knowledge of project management and the required leadership competencies.

The organization should recognize project management as a task for professional project managers. Develop a project management competency framework and an official career path to help project managers grow in the role.

STAKEHOLDERS

Stakeholders are individuals and groups (entities, organizations, etc.) that are impacted by, are involved in or have an interest in the outcome of a project. The larger the project, the more stakeholders there will likely be. The more stakeholders, the more efforts required in terms of communication and change management activities.

Most humans need stability to feel at ease. Yet many projects bring changes to the status quo. Therefore, resistance to the project should always be assumed, especially in projects introducing significant changes into the organization. The larger the number of people against the project, the more difficult it will be to achieve. The same is true for powerful persons who are against the project. In the project world, the following aphorism is well known: "There is always someone who will be happy if your project fails. Find them and understand why." On the other hand, identifying those stakeholders that are most powerful and convincing them of the value of the project for the organization can help to accelerate and gain executive support for a struggling project.

EXAMPLE

In the case of Berlin Brandenburg International Willy Brandt Airport (see chapter one for details), the stakeholders were the state of Brandenburg, the German federal government, the city mayor, the airlines, the passengers, the workers, the citizens of Berlin and the two other Berlin airports. In contrast, we could assume that some of the key stakeholders at Berlin's Tegel and Schönefeld airports didn't mind the massive delays that the Brandenburg project has, and continues to, experience.

The more stakeholders, the more complex the project and the more effort required in communication and change management matters. Also, projects that challenge the status quo will often face quite some resistance.

In this case, an upfront identification of the key stakeholders would have helped the project team to understand the stakeholders' needs and interests in the project. In any project, if the resistance is too strong, it is likely that the rationale for the project is not clear enough.

To be compelling, it has to address the needs of the groups and people impacted by the project. In certain instances, if there is not enough buy-in from key players, it is better to postpone or not to start the project. Berlin Brandenburg Airport is a good example of a project that should not have started until full engagement from key parties was secured.

KEY QUESTIONS TO ASK

- How many stakeholders does the project have?
- Can you identify any major resistance that might bring the project down?

TOOLS TO USE

Stakeholder analysis matrix: This matrix is the most frequently used for weighing and balancing the interests of those who are impacted by or involved in the changes a project will bring about. Whenever possible, address their needs to meet the project's objectives. As opposed to the risk appraisal, which should be carried out with a larger group, stakeholder analysis should be performed in a smaller group, as some of the discussions can be quite sensitive.

The initial assessment is usually performed during the preparation phase by the project leader with the project sponsor. After the major stakeholders have been identified, each one is categorized according to two dimensions. The first is the level of interest (positive or negative) in the project or its outcome. The second is the level of influence (positive or negative) that the stakeholder could have on the project. Usually this dimension is linked to the power of the individual or group in the organization. The third is using the colour coding RAG (red, amber and green) to indicate the stakeholder's current position towards the project.

The analysis can be done on a regular basis to track the changes in stakeholders' attitudes over time. FIGURE 12 (on the next page) is an example of a stakeholder matrix that you can use as a basis to identify and address the stakeholders impacted by and involved in your project.

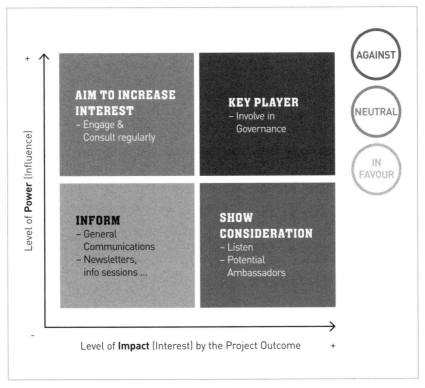

FIGURE 12.

Project stakeholder analysis matrix

WHAT TO DO TO ENSURE PROJECT SUCCESS

The shift from hard project management skills to soft and the increase in the complexity of projects have make stakeholder management one of the areas that requires the most attention. Understanding the needs of the key stakeholders, identifying win–wins and aligning stakeholders to actively support the project are key for project success but can be daunting tasks. The project manager needs to engage the executive sponsor, who plays a major role in stakeholder management.

CHANGE MANAGEMENT

Change management is about ensuring that the organization and its employees are ready to embrace the changes introduced by a project. Communication is one of the most important aspects. Based on the stakeholder analysis, the project manager needs to define the types of information that will be delivered, who will receive it, the format for communicating it, and the timing of its release and distribution. According to PMI's Guide to the Project Management Body of Knowledge, about 75-90% of a project manager's time is spent formally or informally communicating during the implementation phase of a project.[88]

According to the PMI's *Pulse of the Profession* report (an annual global survey about trends in project management), highly effective communicators are more likely to deliver projects on time and within budget.[89]

To advance a project, it is important that everybody gets the right messages at the right times. The first step is to find out what kind of information and/or intervention each stakeholder group needs to embrace the changes introduced by the project. It is often about informing them about the reality and the status of the project, not about painting a rosy picture of the future. Communications to stakeholders may consist of either good news or bad news.

Nowadays, technology has a major impact on how people are kept in the loop. Methods of change management can take many forms, such as written updates, newsletters, face-to-face meetings, presentations, town halls, training sessions, a project website, and so on and so on.

The main challenge is not to bury stakeholders in too much information, but you do want to give them enough so that they're informed and can make appropriate decisions.

EXAMPLE

One of the best examples I remember of change management happened during the introduction of the euro. On 1 January 1999, the EU introduced its new currency, the euro. Originally, the euro was an overarching currency used for exchange between countries within the union, while each nation continued to use its own currency. Within three years, however, the euro was established as an everyday currency and had replaced the domestic currencies of the member states of the Eurozone. During the years prior to the introduction, as well as during the transition, almost all European citizens knew about the project and were fully prepared for the change. Their backgrounds, nationalities, ages and other characteristics didn't matter – they knew the key dates and the benefits the euro would bring to them, and they even knew the conversation rate between their existing currency and the euro.

The project had two key success factors. First, getting the population of Europe ready for the change and communication were top priorities for the European leaders. Second, the project was done in an extremely simple way, so that every single citizen, no matter their education and culture, would understand the purpose, benefits, implications and timing of the euro conversion project.

KEY QUESTIONS TO ASK
- Does the project have a communication and change management plan that highlights the expected benefits for the stakeholders?
- Have sufficient communication and change management activities been planned to support the organization or country with the new reality?

TOOLS TO USE
The European Commission (EC) developed a detailed change management plan, in every language of the EU, which included information packs, visuals, commercials, toolkits and so on. Here are some examples that you can use as a basis for your transformation projects:
- Preparing the Introduction of the Euro: A Short Handbook[90]
- Communication Toolkit.[91]

In addition, the EC created a comprehensive website that included all relevant information. Most of the communication material has been used every time new member states have joined the euro.

WHAT TO DO TO ENSURE PROJECT SUCCESS

All projects require a sound change management plan and communications plan, but not all projects will have the same types of activities or the same methods for distributing and communicating the information. The project plan should document the types of information and change needs the stakeholders have, when the information should be distributed or needs addressed, and how the interventions will be delivered.

It is necessary to prioritize the change and communication activities and convey the right amount of information. Too much communication can be overwhelming, leading to important information getting lost. On the other hand, too little communication might not provide a clear enough picture to allow team members to complete the work that needs to be done. Project managers who understand how to send the right amount of information to the right people at the right time will be able to keep things moving smoothly, resulting in a successful project.

DOMAIN 4: WHERE

The **Where** domain covers the external elements that can have a positive or negative impact on the project. These areas are often outside the control of the project leader, yet there are ways that the leader can influence the project favourably. The executive sponsor plays an important role in influencing the organization too.

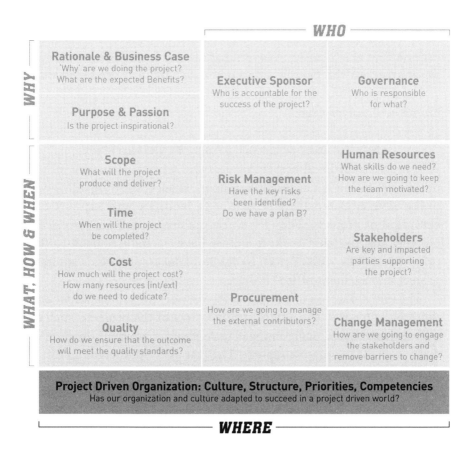

FIGURE 13.
Project Canvas – Domain 4: Where

PROJECT-DRIVEN ORGANIZATION

Most Western companies have a hierarchical, functional structure, which is ideal for running their daily business activities. Budgets, resources, key performance indicators and decision power are 'owned' by the heads of business units, departments and functions.

However, the largest and most critical projects – the strategic ones – are cross-functional and cross-hierarchical by nature: they cut across the organization. This means that a strategic project, such as expanding the business into another country, requires resources and input from a number of different departments and functions. Facilities experts find the location, lawyers handle the legal documents, HR experts recruit the people, salespeople develop a commercial plan and so forth. Without the contributions of all these departments, the project will not succeed.

A KEY ELEMENT OF A PROJECT-DRIVEN ORGANIZATION

Within the traditional hierarchical organizational structure, quick project execution is not possible. The most successful organizations today have adjusted their structure to facilitate and support the execution of projects. They have become project driven: resources, budgets and decision-making power have partially shifted to the project activities, often driven by the implementation of a corporate project management office (PMO).

The initial purpose of a PMO was to support the project leader and the project team in the administrative tasks of the projects, such as tracking timesheets, maintaining issue logs and chasing information in order to provide progress reports. The role evolved towards an office in charge of the development and implementation of policies and standards on project management. This strong focus on 'administrative tasks' created a negative perception of the value of these PMOs, which commonly led to them being dismantled.

The new version of the PMO has a stronger focus on value creation. They are now linked to the executive team. Their role has evolved and now includes promoting and establishing best practices, building competencies, supporting the top levels of management in prioritizing projects, and executing the most strategic projects. The most advanced PMOs have a series of project managers, often the best in the company, who are in charge of leading the most complex and transversal (company-wide) initiatives. Often the office reports to the CEO, so it is sometimes called a CEO office. Most of the large organizations today have one.

A great example of the power of the PMO comes from a leading Swiss biotech company. The CEO's goal was to grow revenues by €1 billion by 2022. He established a transformation PMO and selected one of the brightest people in the management team to lead it. She reported to the CEO. The executive team, with the support of the PMO head, selected 13 strategic initiatives. They appointed the most talented people, who received extensive executive training. Nine out of the 13 initiatives are on track and starting to deliver some benefits, and the company is on course to deliver the CEO's target.

PRIORITIZATION

Projects that are top priority for an organization or country always have a better chance of being delivered successfully. For example, projects relating to the introduction of the General Data Protection Regulation (GDPR) in 2018, which had a fixed deadline and mandatory adherence, were high priority in most organizations. The regulation aims to give control of their personal data to EU citizens. Companies knew they needed to comply to avoid punishment, so managers readily committed resources to the project.

Prioritizing increases the success rates of strategic projects, increases the alignment and focus of senior management teams around strategic goals, clears all doubts for the operational teams when faced with decisions, and, most importantly, builds an execution mindset and culture.

Despite the importance of having a prioritized list of projects, the reality is that most organizations and governments struggle to prioritize. Many don't even have a list of all the projects they are carrying out. Prioritization means saying 'no' to many potential ideas, or cancelling projects previously started. Most successful companies clearly know what are their top projects and are extremely disciplined in those projects' execution.

One of the most challenging aspects of prioritization is that often all of the potential projects and ideas do make sense, yet there are constraints regarding resources and budgets. Even more importantly, the more projects there are, the harder it is to deliver them successfully.

Most companies only prioritize when they enter a crisis and are on the brink of collapse. Famous examples are Apple, LEGO, the Ford Motor Company, Boeing, Philips and Unilever. Only when the executive teams put pressure on these companies were they able to scrap hundreds of projects and products, and focus on the ones that were essential – often the ones that had made the company successful.

To explain the strategic relevance of prioritization and assist executives in the process, I developed a model called the Hierarchy of Purpose,[92] which is explained in detail in chapter eight.

CAPABILITIES

Consistently excelling in project execution requires strong project management capabilities. Resources dedicated to leading projects have to be trained and certified, with the role considered as a profession. A career path and a training development programme are also musts.

Being a successful project manager today does not only require strong project management capabilities. **Technical** skills, such as planning, scoping and risk management, are a given but are not enough. Due to the increase in the complexity in organizations, project managers need to develop all of the following:

- solid **leadership** capabilities, such as communication, persuasion, an executive mindset and negotiation skills
- a good understanding of the **business and the environment** the organization is operating within; the strategy of the firm, the competition, the products and/or services, operations and technology – all are important elements that the project manager should be aware of. Basically, project managers are becoming project and business leaders.

The Swiss biotech company I referred to earlier engaged one of the leading executive education schools to design a tailor-made development programme for its most talented soon-to-be project leaders.

The programme's backbone was project management, but it also included leadership, finance, team development and communication sessions. Additionally, it incorporated several sessions on the biotech's own business (e.g. new products in the pipeline) and about the technological future. It required strong commitment from the participants, as it was run over three sets of four day-sessions held over the course of a year. It was a huge investment for the company but a great development opportunity. It clearly showed the CEO's firm commitment to investing in talent to deliver his ambition through project excellence.

KEY QUESTIONS TO ASK
- Does the organization have a PMO that strategically supports the selection, prioritization and execution of projects?
- Is the project a priority for the company?
- Does the organization have a career path and development programme to groom project leaders and build project execution capabilities?

WHAT TO DO TO ENSURE PROJECT SUCCESS
It is important that the organization's structure is adapted to support the execution of projects. Power and resources have to be shifted, with the organization moving from the hierarchical model to the project model. The PMO should be established at corporate level and be empowered by the CEO. Shifting the structure also means creating a career path and development program for project managers.

HOW TO APPLY THE PROJECT
CANVAS IN YOUR PROJECTS
AND IN YOUR ORGANIZATION

Fundamental transformations, such as changing a company's values and culture, always require a big investment of time, money and effort, and their benefits are very difficult to quantify. Often, the benefits are of the so-called soft – or intangible – variety, such as an improvement in motivation or the creation of an entrepreneurial mindset. The hard benefits, such as cost savings or revenue increases, are frequently not concrete. In addition, gains are generally achieved in the medium to long term, usually after three to five years of hard work.

Because CEOs and top management receive substantial pressure from shareholders and the stock markets to quickly and regularly show positive returns on their investments, they tend to be reluctant to embark on these types of initiative. Instead, they prefer to invest in acquisitions or downsizing projects, which pay off much more quickly and have a tangible impact on the bottom line.

Introducing the Project Canvas in your organization should not be as complicated as a transformation project, but it does require some radical changes in the way projects are proposed, selected, prioritized, defined, planned and executed.

A simple and agile approach I like to use to start moving towards a project-driven organization is increasing project consistency by following these **seven implementation steps**:

1. Develop a standard set of terms and definitions relating to projects.
2. Develop a common project guideline based on the Project Canvas.
3. Develop training for executive sponsors.
4. Develop training for project leaders.
5. Select the most qualified and enthusiastic people to be project ambassadors.

6. Assign them the most relevant and/or strategic projects.
7. Strive to become a project-driven organization.

In addition, apply the following golden rules at any time to assess your and/or your organization's project capabilities:

- Push back on ideas until they are mature enough to launch a full-scale project.
- Senior executives should dedicate at least 20% of their time to supporting a project they are sponsoring.
- Projects should have an ambitious SMART goal with a clear fixed deadline.
- The best resources should be allocated to the best projects. They should be taken out of their full-time job and allowed to dedicate 100% of their time to the project.
- Quality – testing, iterations – of the end product or solution should be an obsession.

PROJECTS @WORK

UNDERSTANDING GREAT
PROJECTS THAT CHANGED THE
WORLD THROUGH THE LENS
OF THE PROJECT CANVAS.

My purpose is to share a positive view of projects and provide the basic skills and framework for everyone to succeed in the new project-driven world. There are thousands of amazing examples of great projects: projects that have transformed countries, projects that have changed organizations and projects that have had an incredible impact on humanity. Unfortunately, they often pass by unnoticed. One reason for this is that dramatic failures involving large amounts of money are naturally interesting. We all love a big flop – especially one that has been talked up as a huge boon for humanity. Most of the project literature is about failed projects, big disasters, humongous cost overruns and delays. This book aims at changing that: shifting the focus to the positive side of projects.

In my search for world-class examples, I found startling projects that have transformed entire countries, regions and organizations. The greatest governments and political leaders have been big promoters of projects, and this is also the case for businesses and corporations with visionary leaders. These great leaders launched and drove ambitious projects linked to an inspirational vision and a deeper purpose; designed and implemented with precision, applying the concepts that made projects successful; and delivered astonishing lasting benefits, not only financial but also social.

Interestingly, I also found that countries and regions that didn't have a predominantly long-term vision, with clear goals and projects, often ended up in political instability and social chaos. Notorious cases of this shortage of vision and projects are the unpredictable political situations occurring in Spain, Italy, the UK and even the US as of this writing in 2018. And the same applies to businesses and corporations: those that forget or don't dare to invest in projects tend to disappear.

Some of the most spectacular projects in history have been triggered by global urbanization – the move from rural areas to cities, accelerated by the industrial revolution and decreasing mortality rates through improvements in healthcare systems. Urbanization leads to changes in economic activities and lifestyle. The industrialization of coastal China and its integration into the global trade system have led to the largest rural-to-urban migration in history, entailing a rise in urban population from 191 million in 1980, to 622 million in 2009.[93]

Cities account for the bulk of production, distribution and consumption. Over the past 50 years, metropoles such as London, Paris, New York, Mexico City, Sao Paolo, Shanghai and Tokyo have implemented millions of construction, infrastructure, transportation, educational and social projects. With more than half of the global population living in cities, the focus of projects has shifted in areas such as urban mobility, smart cities, environment and sustainable matters.

Let's look at some remarkable projects and analyse them through the new lens of the Project Canvas.

ICELAND: TO BANKRUPTCY AND BACK

The financial crisis of 2008 impacted every Western country, but none as hard as in Iceland, the isolated island with a population of 300,000 and unique natural resources. Relative to the size of its economy, Iceland's crisis was the biggest in the world. The three largest banks in the country – Glitnir, Landsbanki and Kaupthing – had assets ten times as large as Iceland's annual GDP.[94]

Iceland responded to its meltdown in the opposite way from the rest of Europe. In a climate where banks were deemed 'too big to fail', Iceland found that its three big banks were in fact 'too big to save'.[95] The banks collapsed and were split into domestic and foreign parts, with the government guaranteeing domestic deposits while abandoning the foreign parts. It allowed its currency to fall in value – the króna was allowed to depreciate by almost 60% from the end of 2007 to 2008, restoring competitiveness and flipping the trade balance into a surplus. In 2009, capital controls were introduced to put a floor on the currency and contain inflation. And Iceland was the only country in which bank executives in connection with the crisis went to jail – as many as 26 of them.[96] This was a strong and symbolic message that closed the past and looked towards a new future.

Today, Iceland has fully recovered from the crash, and its economy is one of the best performing in the developed world, with a 7% growth rate. Iceland has diversified from fish, tourism and aluminium into renewable energy and information technology. And, more importantly, the country's income inequality levels, measured by the Gini coefficient, are back to levels seen before the financial bubble, thanks to the government's policies to protect the lower income classes.

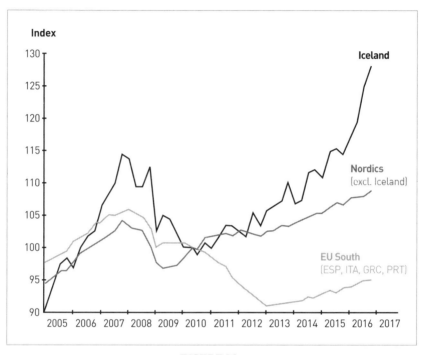

FIGURE 14.

Real GDP growth in Iceland, compared with the Nordic countries and the southern area of the European Union

Source: Organisation for Economic Co-operation and Development

What is fascinating about this spectacular project is that the citizens' will drove it to success. Social movements used the crisis as a trigger to become a better, less corrupt, more diversified and more equal nation. The revival plan was designed in 2009 by the Social Democratic Party and Green Party coalition.[97] The project was then implemented by an alliance between Independence Party and the Progressive Party. The government more or less followed the course set out in the International

Monetary Fund's programme, which included the imposition of capital controls and other financial measures in exchange for a loan of $5 billion to serve its external financing needs.[98] One major reason for the success was Iceland's ownership of the programme: politicians and leading civil servants made great efforts to reach the goals set out in the programme.

ICELAND: RECONSTRUCTION PROJECT (2008–2018)
PROJECT CANVAS

WHY: RATIONALE, BUSINESS CASE, PURPOSE AND PASSION
- Survival and recovery of Iceland after its bankruptcy
- Create a better country – more equal, diversified, free of corruption

WHO: ACCOUNTABILITY AND GOVERNANCE
- The Social Democrats and Green Party actively sponsored the recovery
- The true force behind the project was a social movement led by Iceland's citizens
- Politicians and civil servants made great efforts to reach the goals set in the programme

WHAT, HOW & WHEN: HARD AND SOFT ASPECTS OF THE PROJECT
- Iceland responded to its meltdown in the opposite way from the rest of Europe
- The International Monetary Fund set out a $2.1 billion support program with three clear objectives
- There was 100% buy-in from the citizens (key stakeholders)
- Ten years later, Iceland is one of the best-performing economies in the developed world (7% growth)

WHERE: ORGANIZATION, CULTURE, CONTEXT AND COMPETENCIES
- Survival situation, urgency to change
- Priority number one project that received all the attention and resources needed

RWANDA: THE MOST INCREDIBLE RECONCILIATION PROGRAMME EVER

In 1994, Rwanda suffered one of the most atrocious genocides that recent history remembers. Up to 1 million people perished in three months and as many as 250,000 women were raped, leaving the country's population traumatized, its infrastructure decimated, and its judicial and political system completely annihilated.

In the late 1990s, President Paul Kagame and his government started to look at their country in a different way. They began actively planning methods and established a Vision 2020 programme,[99] composed of 44 goals.

Since then, Rwanda has embarked on an ambitious development and reconciliation process with the ultimate aim of all Rwandans once again living side by side in peace. The Constitution now states that all Rwandans share equal rights. Laws have been passed to fight discrimination and a divisive, genocidal ideology.

Primary responsibility for reconciliation efforts rested in a new body, the National Unity and Reconciliation Commission,[100] established in 1999. The main activities performed by this body were around awareness and education. Several studies were carried out investigating the sources of the division and conflicts, and how to mitigate them in the future. National summits were organized around human rights, national history, good governance. Training on conflict management and trauma counselling was provided to women, adolescents and political leaders. Peace education programs (Ingando), explaining the origins of the division and Rwandan's history were provided. A leadership academy (Itorero) was established to develop leaders and promote Rwanda's values. From 2007 to 2009, 115,228 participants took part in the Itorero programme.[101]

So far, the results of this transformation programme have been extraordinary, particularly in light of the terrible devastation the country found itself in 1994.

The National Unity and Reconciliation Commission has twice released a 'reconciliation barometer', which looks at dozens of factors to determine how well people are living together. In 2015, the last year for which the figures are available, the country deemed reconciliation in Rwanda to be at 92.5%.[102]

One of the most remarkable aspects of the Vision 2020 programme was its aim to eradicate the high levels of corruption present in the country, one of the major obstacles to prosperity and one of the main factors that led to the genocide. To win the fight against corruption, the programme's leaders learned from Singapore the importance that cleanliness can have in influencing citizens and the overall culture of a country. The logic behind this is the idea that, if a city is clean, its government and politics will be clean too. Kigali, the capital of Rwanda, is one of the cleanest cities in the world. Corruption levels have dropped by half, with the result that Rwanda has become one of the least corrupt countries in Africa (advancing from 83rd to 49th place according to Transparency International).[103]

FIGURE 15.
Kigali, one of the cleanest capitals in Africa

Rwanda's Vision 2020 programme has achieved a number of other improvements too. For example, literacy grew from 48% in 1995 to just over 71% in 2016[104]. And in 2016 women held 56% of seats in parliament – one of the largest percentages in the world.

RWANDA: RECONSTRUCTION AND RECONCILIATION PROGRAMME (1994–2014)
PROJECT CANVAS

WHY: RATIONALE, BUSINESS CASE, PURPOSE AND PASSION
- Recover country after one of the worst genocides in recent history
- Reduce rampant levels of corruption
- Improve quality of living of Rwandese citizens

WHO: ACCOUNTABILITY AND GOVERNANCE
- President Paul Kagame actively sponsored the reconstruction and reconciliation
- The National Unity and Reconciliation Commission was established to follow up all projects

WHAT, HOW & WHEN: HARD AND SOFT ASPECTS OF THE PROJECT
- The Vision 2020 programme set the framework for Rwanda's development
- The country invested heavily in the education of its political leaders
- There was a great focus on communication and interaction with the population (seminars, training, etc.)
- Despite the reluctance of the citizens after the genocide, they became very supportive

WHERE: ORGANIZATION, CULTURE, CONTEXT AND COMPETENCIES
- Country devastated; there was an urgent need to reform
- Priority number one project that received all the attention and resources needed

CURITIBA, BRAZIL: BECOMING THE GREENEST CITY ON EARTH

Curitiba has become the gold standard in sustainable urban planning, variously called the "green capital", the "greenest city on earth" and the "most innovative city in the world".

For quite a long time, Curitiba was a transit city; workers would stop by on their way to the agricultural areas. The city had a several influxes of migration from European nationals searching for work and a better life. Throughout 1940 and 1960, the city's population dramatically increased – from 140,000 to 360,000 inhabitants.[105] With the increase of population, the number of cars increased too. Curitiba was becoming chaotic, with huge traffic jams around the city center and surroundings.

It all started with one man and a simple idea: "Prioritizing people over cars."[106] Jaime Lerner[107] had studied architecture and urban planning, but he had great interest in politics. He became the mayor of Curitiba in the early 1970s.

During the first months, he was presented with an urbanization project that would follow the steps of Brasilia, the capital of Brazil, aiming at augmenting the primary avenues of the downtown area to adapt to expanded traffic sacrificing all buildings and green spaces.

Yet, Lerner actually did the opposite of what had been suggested: paving the streets and closing them to traffic, creating Brazil's first pedestrian mall in 1972. The project faced big resistance from the locals. Mayor Lerner forced the situation and ordered that it had to be executed over 72 hours.

This project summarizes Lerner's management approach: act now, adjust later.

But Lerner and his team had bigger plans for the city. He wanted to transform mobility and urban transportation through implementing low-budget ideas and projects. One of his most famous quotes, rather unusual among public servants, is: "If you want creativity, cut one zero from the budget. If you want sustainability, cut two zeros."[108]

By 1974, the city had introduced a new street design that provided express lanes for buses. Passengers could board buses from new stations along the middle of the city's main streets, allowing buses to move uninterrupted through the city. But, in the late 1980s, Lerner noticed that the inflow and outflow of passengers were slowing down the speeds of the buses at each station.

Three innovations followed: a new system of raised platforms (the futuristic tube station system for which Curitiba has grown famous) that allow passengers to move straight from the station into the bus without the hassle of stairs; longer buses to add extra capacity to the fleet; and a system of pre-payment so that bus drivers do not have to issue tickets and collect money on the go.

FIGURE 16.
The Bus Rapid Transit system

Lerner's measures had significant impact: today, roughly 85% of Curitiba uses the Bus Rapid Transit system, which transports roughly 2 million passengers each day (for comparison, the London Underground system carries 3 million).

In parallel to the urban transformation projects, Lerner and his team also focused on green projects, developing parks and city gardens. Back in 1971, Curitiba had only one park; today, the city has 16 parks, 14 forests and more than 1,000 green public spaces. It now has five times the amount of green space recommended by the World Health Organization – which suggests a minimum of 9m^2 of green space per capita – per inhabitant. It has more than 50 square metres of green space per person compared with neighbouring Buenos Aires's 2 square metres.

According to Mayor Lerner, "Politics is about providing a collective dream" and about "creating a scenario that everyone can understand and see is desirable. Then they will help you make it happen."[109]

FIGURE 17.
Barigui Park in Curitiba

CURITIBA: SUSTAINABLE TRANSFORMATION PROGRAMME (1972–2007)
PROJECT CANVAS

WHY: RATIONALE, BUSINESS CASE, PURPOSE AND PASSION
- Transform a fast-growing city into one of the world's greenest and most sustainable cities
- Improve urban and transport planning to increase use and reduce commute time
- Create parks and green spaces: make the city a leisure paradise

WHO: ACCOUNTABILITY AND GOVERNANCE
- Mayor Jaime Lerner was actively engaged as sponsor of the transformation
- The Curitiba Research and Urban Planning Institute was in charge of following up the projects

WHAT, HOW & WHEN: HARD AND SOFT ASPECTS OF THE PROJECT
- Mayor Jaime Lerner had a strong vision and will to create a unique city
- Lerner's planning philosophy was to act now and adjust later to overcome resistance to change
- Emphasis was placed on communicating the vision and the benefits to engage Curitiba's population

WHERE: ORGANIZATION, CULTURE, CONTEXT AND COMPETENCIES
- The quick wins in the first projects created a positive culture throughout the city
- Curitiba's transformation was top priority, thus receiving sufficient resources
- External expertise (e.g. the Japanese architect Hitoshi Nakamura) was used to create the green spaces

6. PROJECTS@WORK

SWEDEN: TRAFFIC SWITCHING SIDES, THE LARGEST LOGISTICAL PROJECT IN SWEDISH HISTORY

Sunday 3 September 1967 was by far the largest logistical event in Sweden's history,[110] better known as H-Day (from 'Högertrafikom-läggningen' in Swedish, referring to the right-hand traffic diversion). On that day, millions of Swedes changed from driving on the left side to driving on the right. It was the reversal of a 230 year old driving system, and probably the largest revamp in driving infrastructure seen in history.

Many Swedes who travelled by car to their neighbouring Scandina-vian countries – Norway, Denmark and Finland were driving on the right-hand side – got into car accidents because of their unfamiliarity with the traffic system. The same happened to tourists who came by car to Sweden.

Swedish automotive companies, in particular Volvo, made cars to be driven on the right so they could more easily be exported to the rest of the right-hand-driving world. Yet many of these cars were purchased and driven in Sweden. Paradoxically, approximately 90% of Swedes drove vehicles designed to be driven on the right. There were 1.5 million cars on the roads and this number was expected to reach 2.8 million by 1975.[111]

The switch idea had been discussed for decades. A nationwide referendum carried out in 1955 on the proposal concluded with 83% of the voters against the change. In 1963, after years of strong lobbying, the parliament approved the proposal of Prime Minister Tage Erlander for the introduction of right-hand-drive traffic in 1967.

To prepare the country and define the details of the project, a dedicated office – the Statens Högertrafikkommission (State Right-Hand Traffic Commission) – was established, along with the Swedish National Traffic Safety Board. The project had a very detailed preparation phase. It included the creation of a four-year education programme, with advice from psychologists, to ensure that the entire population was prepared for the change and aware of how they could participate on the day of the switchover. Among the initiatives taken

127

by the government to support the change were a communications campaign that displayed the H-Day logo on various commemorative items, and a television contest involving songs about the change.

FIGURE 18.

The logo used by the campaign to promote H-Day

A few days before the conversion, every intersection was equipped with an extra set of poles and traffic signals wrapped in black plastic, and new road markings were painted on the roads with white paint, then covered with black tape.

On 3 September 1967 – H-Day – the country was ready for the switch. All non-essential traffic was banned from the roads from 1am to 6am. During that timeframe, construction teams performed the final infrastructural changes. At 4.50am the new road signs were revealed and the cars were rerouted to the opposite side.

The relatively smooth changeover saw a reduction in the number of accidents. On the day of the change, only minor accidents were reported. One week after some improvements were already noticed: 125 reported traffic accidents, none of them fatal, compared with 130 to 198 before the change. According to traffic experts, as people already drove vehicles designed to be driven on the right side of the road – providing a better view of the road ahead – the number of accidents that occurred while people were overtaking reduced. The numbers of fatal car-to-car and car-to-pedestrian accidents dropped sharply as a result, and the number of motor insurance claims went down by 40%.[112]

Sweden's successful shift to the right was made possible through government hand-holding, with massive publicity and public education campaigns meant to prepare the population running for at least a year in advance.

SWEDEN: TRAFFIC SWITCHES SIDES (1967)
PROJECT CANVAS

WHY: RATIONALE, BUSINESS CASE, PURPOSE AND PASSION
- Reduction of traffic accidents and facilitate left-seated driving
- Align with the neighbouring countries and most of the rest of the world

WHO: ACCOUNTABILITY AND GOVERNANCE
- Prime Minister Tage Erlander was the top sponsor of the project
- The Swedish National Traffic Safety Board and State Right-Hand Traffic Commission followed up on the programme

WHAT, HOW & WHEN: HARD AND SOFT ASPECTS OF THE PROJECT
- There was a fixed deadline: 3 September 1967
- There was detailed and precise preparation
- The government organized massive communication and public education campaigns

WHERE: ORGANIZATION, CULTURE, CONTEXT AND COMPETENCIES
- Every Swedish citizen was made aware of the change and its implications
- Priority number one project that received all the attention and resources needed

EURO CONVERSION: A 300-MILLION-PEOPLE TRANSFORMATION

For most Europeans, the euro is part of daily life, yet the conversion to the euro was one of the largest political, social and economic transformations in history. Mobilizing more than 300 million European citizens and changing one of the key components of their day-to-day lives is not a common endeavour. Today, the euro is shared by as many as 340 million Europeans in 19 member states, and it has become the second most used currency around the world.[113]

There are all sorts of opinions about whether the consequences of the euro conversion project have been positive or negative. My view is that the euro has been an extraordinary success from the point of view of a massive transformation project. However, the project was part of a larger project, the European Economic and Monetary Union, which is languishing due to the lack of shared vision and poor political leadership.

Accomplishing this huge transformation required an exhaustive ideation phase. In fact, the euro conversion project started more than 20 years before the currency was introduced, with the establishment of the European Monetary System in 1978 which involved creation of the European Currency Unit.[114] It also required thorough preparation and a perfect plan. Around 14 billion notes and 52 billion coins were produced, of which some 7.8 billion notes and 40 billion coins were distributed at the beginning of January 2002 to 218,000 banks and post offices, 2.8 million sales outlets, and 302 million individuals in the 12 participating countries. In parallel, a large proportion of the 9 billion national notes and 107 billion national coins in circulation were withdrawn.[115]

If we analyse the project through the lens of the Project Canvas, we see that every single element was perfectly thought through and planned, and seamlessly executed.

The euro was created in the provisions of the 1992 Maastricht Treaty. A clear vision, rationale and benefits were set from the outset: to bring Europeans closer together, to help integrate and boost prosperity among the member states. This vision not only touched citizens' heads but also their hearts.

A clear system of governance was established, with the Council of the European Union, which represents the executive governments of the EU's member states, as the key decision-making and oversight body, acting as a de facto steering committee. The creation of the European Central Bank, on 1 June 1998, provided the executing body of the project, and it later became the administrator of the monetary policy of the Eurozone.

The scope and requirements were clearly defined through what were termed the 'convergence criteria': to participate in the currency, member states had to meet five strict criteria, such as having a budget deficit of less than 3% of their GDP, and price stability.

The timings were outlined and cast in stone. The currency was introduced, in non-physical form, at midnight on 1 January 1999, when the national currencies of the participating states ceased to exist independently. Their exchange rates were locked at fixed rates against each other.

To manage the unprecedented colossal risks and allow people, companies and organizations to make the necessary adjustments, a prolonged transition of three years was established. However, the notes and coins of the old currencies continued to be used as legal tender until the new euro coins and banknotes were launched on 1 January 2002, when the biggest cash changeover in history took place, involving 12 EU countries (Austria, Belgium, Finland, France, Germany, Greece, Ireland, Italy, Luxembourg, the Netherlands, Portugal and Spain). The changeover period (during which the former currencies' notes and coins were exchanged for those of the euro) lasted about two months, until 28 February 2002.

One of the key elements of this massive project was the active engagement of all the stakeholders, combined with a strong investment in change management and communication activities. Despite those stakeholders consisting of more than 300 million citizens and thousands of impacted parties (institutions, companies, banks, etc.), most of their needs were proactively addressed through extensive communication campaigns, information kits, help desks, training sessions and other means.

The success of this huge transformation project was due to the thorough preparations made, the active participation of all sectors involved and the enthusiasm of the public.

EURO CONVERSION PROJECT (1999–2002)
PROJECT CANVAS

WHY: RATIONALE, BUSINESS CASE, PURPOSE AND PASSION
- Further integration between European nations
- More prosperity for Europe and its citizens

WHO: ACCOUNTABILITY AND GOVERNANCE
- The Council of the European Union (formed of the member states' heads) acted as a de facto steering committee
- The European Central Bank acted as the implementation body

WHAT, HOW & WHEN: HARD AND SOFT ASPECTS OF THE PROJECT
- There was a fixed deadline: 1 January 2002
- There was a clear scope: five convergence criteria
- Massive communication and public education campaigns were undertaken

WHERE: ORGANIZATION, CULTURE, CONTEXT AND COMPETENCIES
- All European citizens were informed and equipped for the transformation
- Priority number one project for the impacted member states, meaning it received all the attention and resources needed

BOEING 777: AN ENGINEERING MARVEL

In the late 1980s, when Boeing announced the development of the 777 (also called the 'Triple Seven'), many aviation experts questioned the need for a new model, since Boeing's 747 had been flying successfully for over 30 years. Some experts suggested that it was cheaper to improve existing features of the 747 to increase efficiency for operators and convenience for passengers, as opposed to developing a completely new aircraft. Designing and developing a new aircraft was a huge investment and a massively complex endeavour.

Airplane manufacturers, like auto manufacturers, had to keep innovating by introducing new airplane models if they wanted to survive in the competitive world. To cut costs on designing and developing the new 777 model, Boeing, under the leadership of Alan Mulally, adopted an innovative and collaborative designing and development process that involved customers, air carriers, technicians, finance experts, computer experts and even other aircraft manufacturers.

The budget was over $6 billion and more than 10,000 people worked on the project. The manufacturing facilities were covering an area equivalent to over 70 soccer fields.

The 777 would be designed using the latest three-dimensional digital imaging technology.[116] The plane would be powered by lighter twin engines, the most powerful ever built, and designed to be 20% more fuel efficient than its precursors. The frame, some of which was constructed with new materials, would add to its efficient use of fuel.

With this project, Boeing aimed at achieving three strategic objectives:
- reduce aircraft development time significantly
- meet customers' requirements better by involving them in the development process
- eliminate costly modification procedures.

A key innovation introduced in the 777 project was to share the financial risk. Boeing would manufacture the flight deck, forward section of the cabin, wings, tail and engine nacelles (casing) in its own plants, while it would subcontract the rest of the components (about 70%) to suppliers around the world. The vendors that participated in the project were Alenia in Italy, ASTA in Australia, BAE Systems in the UK, Bombardier Shorts in the UK, Embraer in Brazil, various Japanese aerospace companies, Kaman in the US, Korean Air, Northrop Grumman in the US and Singapore Aerospace.[117]

Mulally was determined to introduce new working dynamics in the project. The design phase for the new twinjet was different from that for Boeing's previous commercial jetliners. For the first time, eight major airlines – All Nippon Airways, American Airlines, British Airways, Cathay Pacific, Delta Air Lines, Japan Airlines, Qantas and United Airlines – had a role in the development. This was a departure from industry practice, where manufacturers typically designed aircraft with minimal customer input.

By including all contributors, Mulally changed the way teams were configured. They were open to wider participation and included engineers, procurement staff, manufacturing staff, customers and suppliers, all working together on the design, development and manufacturing processes for the 777.

An important aspect of the cultural change introduced by the leadership of the project was the way in which employees were expected to interact with management. Team members were encouraged to bring their concerns to management. If they failed to receive an answer, they were encouraged to take the problem to the next level until they found a solution to their problems.

The 777 first entered commercial service with United Airlines on 7 June 1995. The 777 has received more orders than any other wide-body airliner; as of June 2018, more than 60 customers had placed orders for 1,986 aircraft of all variants, with 1,559 delivered.[118] It has become Boeing's number one best-selling model, surpassing the Boeing 747.

One pilot has been quoted as saying:

A survey was conducted in 1999 and 2000 worldwide. It revealed that the Boeing 777 was preferred by more than 75% who flew aboard the Boeing 777 and Airbus 330/340 airplanes. As a pilot who has flown both types of airplanes, I still prefer the Boeing 777 in terms of comfort and spaciousness.[119]

VIEWS ON THE PROJECT REVOLUTION

PERSONAL CONVERSATION WITH ALAN MULALLY,
EX-CEO OF BOEING AND FORD MOTORS, AND
PROGRAMME DIRECTOR FOR BOEING 777

What kind of project leadership approaches were you applying at Boeing?

Everything that I've learned over the last 37 years at Boeing, and also eight years at Ford, I've summarized in the simple document titled, "Skilled and Motivated Teams Working Together: Principles and Practices". The big points are to include everybody – it's all about people. It's kind of really saying love them up, appreciate them so much, because you have all these talented people around the world that are working – everybody needs to be included.

Come together around a compelling vision for what the airplane or the programme or the business is, a strategy for achieving it, and also a relentless implementation plan, and that's where the business plan review comes from. Then, of course, there are clear performance goals, having one plan, using facts and data, and the biggest one, probably, is that everybody knows the plan, everybody knows the status, and everybody knows the areas that need special attention. And that's where the business plan reviews come in.

You engaged the stakeholders from the beginning of the project, including customers, suppliers, etc. – can you tell us a bit more about that innovative approach?

One of the reasons I believe that Boeing has been successful over the years is that on every airplane programme, and especially on the 777, we've always included the airlines in the actual design of the airplane.

This is because they have so much knowledge about how to operate the airplane, and how it's going to be used, and their reliability requirements, and the maintainability requirements, and how they're going to take care of it, how they're going to fly the airplane, how they're going to maintain the airplane.

So, we actually invite the airlines that want to participate in the launch of the vehicle to join the team. And it's really funny, because at the first, some of the airlines will say, I don't want to be in the same room with our competitor.

And if I'm going to share a lot of my knowledge with you in front of the competitor, is that going to put me at a competitive disadvantage? And I remember one of the airlines in one of the early meetings, we had, like, 12 of the world's best airlines in the same room. And one of the airline leaders said, okay, here's the deal, we want to help Boeing build the best airplane in the world. When we get that best airplane in the world, because we've all contributed to it, then we can compete as airlines.

What was the most difficult part of the 777 project?
I really don't think of it in those terms, because when you operate with these principles and practices, it's all out in the open. So it's not a problem – it's a gem when somebody has an issue.

It's a gem because now you know what the issue is and you're also recognizing that this is an invention, and it's going to be an iterative process, and that's what engineering and design and manufacturing are about, so it's almost like you're legitimizing the process of project management. So it's not all going to go right on the plan – it means that you have a process to uncover the areas that need special attention, and you have a culture where everybody is going to share the areas that need special attention, and work together to solve them.

So it's almost like we can't wait to get to the business plan review every week to see which performance indicators changed and what we need to work on, because now we know that's part of the process and we have legitimized programme and project management, and we can adapt to all of the changes that you're naturally going to see going forward.

There have been a lot of things written about project and programme management, and you have authored a number of them, Antonio, so I think the reason why I'd want to support you is you dedicate your life to programme and project management. I really think it's the future in this business because it's going to be business that actually keeps us moving forward by making products and services that people want and value.

BOEING 777: AN ENGINEERING MARVEL (1989–1995)
PROJECT CANVAS

WHY: RATIONALE, BUSINESS CASE, PURPOSE AND PASSION
- Objectives clear since the beginning: a) create an aircraft 20% more fuel efficient than its precursors; b) reduce aircraft development time; c) increase market share
- Design and build one of the most advanced aircrafts in history

WHO: ACCOUNTABILITY AND GOVERNANCE
- Alan Mulally programme director for Boeing 777, 100% dedicated to the project
- Clear governance and allocation of roles and responsibilities (including clients and suppliers)
- 10.000 individuals working on the project

WHAT, HOW & WHEN: HARD AND SOFT ASPECTS OF THE PROJECT
- Budget estimated at over $6 billion
- Scope: For the first time, eight major airlines had a role in the development.
- Sharing of the financial risk with the key contributors (clients and suppliers)
- Cultural change introduced by the leadership to promote escalation of concerns

WHERE: ORGANIZATION, CULTURE, CONTEXT AND COMPETENCIES
- Top priority for Boeing: project number one
- Fully dedicated resources, budgets and top management attention
- Priority number one project that received all the attention and resources needed

IPHONE PROJECT PURPLE: THE BEST COMMERCIAL PROJECT EVER

One project that stands out is what in 2004 was called Project Purple, the creation of the iPhone. Since its debut in 2007, the iPhone has become both a cultural and an economic phenomenon, replacing the previous market leaders (Blackberry and Nokia) as the most ubiquitous smartphone and turning the entire global telecoms market upside down. And this from a company with no previous significant experience in the mobile industry!

Let's examine Purple Project to better understand why it was seamlessly executed.

EXPERIMENT UNTIL YOU ARE READY TO LAUNCH A FORMAL PROJECT

Like most of Apple's success stories, the iPhone can trace its roots back to Steve Jobs. Shortly after the first iPod was released in 2002, Apple began thinking about a phone. In 2005, a small team negotiated a limited partnership with the mobile network AT&T, then known as Cingular, to develop the product, but it never really picked up. In fact, there were as many as five different phones or phone-related initiatives – from tiny research endeavours to a flop partnership with Motorola on the ROKR[120] phone (which some described as the first iTunes phone) – bubbling up at Apple by the middle of the 2000s.

What is noteworthy is that Steve Jobs didn't launch a formal and full-scale project to develop the first concepts of the iPhone. The ideation phase was kept low profile, with limited investments and small teams experimenting as described above.

Most organizations have the bad habit of launching a full-blown project for every idea they generate, creating a vast quantity of projects that most of the time end up at a dead end wasting precious company resources.

PROJECT SPONSOR: ENGAGED, DEDICATED, DRIVING, INSPIRING ... WHAT ELSE CAN YOU ASK FOR?

Numerous members of the Apple executive team tried, for several years, to convince Jobs that producing a phone was a great idea. But Jobs was sceptical and rejected the idea of setting up a formal project many times. Linked to the previous point, Jobs' attitude shows how an executive sponsor should behave: being a powerful source of inspiration and a fierce curator of good ideas, yet not afraid of rejecting the bad or half-baked ones.

Once Jobs' scepticism was overcome, he was fully engaged and dedicated, on average, approximately 40% of his time to supervising and supporting the different project teams.

Executive sponsors are key to ensuring that resources are allocated to transversal initiatives, that decisions are taken when problems arise, that executives stay aligned and that the organization remains behind the strategic project. There is no area more important for project success that ongoing executive support.

TIME: THE POWER OF A STRETCHED AND FIXED FINISH LINE – A FRANTIC RACE TO MEET AN IMPOSSIBLE GO-LIVE DATE

The iPhone project was officially launched at the end of 2004. More precisely, it was on the late night of 7 November 2004, after receiving an email from vice president Michael Bell, explaining why they really should make the phone, that Steve Jobs said: "Okay, I think we should go do it."

On 29 June 2007, at the annual Macworld trade show, the first iPhone was released. This means it took only two and a half years to produce a revolutionary phone, the first smartphone, by a company that had not produced phones before.

The last months of the project, as Macworld approached, became a frantic race to get the iPhone ready for launch. Anniversaries were missed, vacations cancelled and family lives disrupted. Project Purple is a great example of the power of establishing a fixed deadline: the pressure it creates on the team, ensuring everyone is 100% focused on the project and making them go the extra mile.

RESOURCES: THE MOST TALENTED TEAM EVER,
THE BEST OF THE BEST, WITH FULL-TIME DEDICATION

As mentioned earlier, the Project Purple team was one of the most talented groups of individuals in recent history. The best engineers, the best programmers, the best designers, were selected to join the team. Not only that, the chosen people were fully discharged from all their duties and were assigned full time to the project effective immediately.

Not only the technicians, Jobs decided to include the best senior executives on the project, starting with Jonny Ive, the designer of the iPod and MacBook, putting him in charge of the look of the handset.

And their lives would never be the same – at least, not for the next two and a half years. Not only would they be working overtime to develop the most influential piece of consumer technology of their generation, but they'd be doing little else. Their personal lives would disappear, and they wouldn't be able to talk about what they were working on.

The Purple Project became their life.

QUALITY OBSESSED

Ensuring that the end product exceeded client expectations was one of the biggest fixations of Jobs. Making a phone for a company that had never produced one made the venture an even more daunting task, including the design and quality standards.

The introduction of new technologies, like the touch-screen or the lack of keyboard, required a huge amount of prototyping and multiple iterations to get it right. Despite the time pressure and the fixed deadline to launch the iPhone, at no point was testing or quality sacrificed.

At several points throughout the project, when things were not going well and the quality of the iPhone was not reached, Jobs gave the team an ultimatum. If there were not able to show progress in two weeks, the project would be assigned to another group. And everybody knew that he was not kidding.

MANAGE PROJECT RISK PROACTIVELY

One of the high risks was the fact that Apple had no experience in producing phones. The learning curve could take many more years than initially planned. To address the development risks, the project team looked at the various options. They came up with two main possibilities: (a) transform the celebrated iPod into a phone (the easier path) or (b) transform the established Mac into a small touch-tablet that made calls.

The two phone projects were split into tracks, code-named P1 and P2, respectively. Both were top secret. P1 was the iPod phone. P2 was the still-experimental hybrid of multi-touch technology and Mac software. Instead of choosing one of them and taking the risk of having made the wrong choice, the team decided to work on both prototypes in parallel. This was a proactive way of mitigating one of the major risks of Project Purple.

According to one estimate, Apple spent $150 million developing the iPhone[121] (excluding the cost of the ideation phase). That $150 million certainly ranks Project Purple as one of the best investments ever. Apple sold 1.4 million iPhones in 2007 and more than 201 million units worldwide in 2016.[122] In total, Apple sold more than 1 billion iPhones worldwide between 2007 and 2016.

In the first quarter of 2017, iPhone sales accounted for more than 69% of Apple's total revenue, with an estimated margin above 50%, generating more than $54 billion in revenues. Apple's revenue grew from $8 billion in 2004 to more than $215 billion in 2016.[123]

IPHONE: PROJECT PURPLE (2004–2007)
PROJECT CANVAS

WHY: RATIONALE, BUSINESS CASE, PURPOSE AND PASSION
- To create a phone that was simple and that people would love
- To make a bet on the future of Apple, entering a new high-growth market

WHO: ACCOUNTABILITY AND GOVERNANCE
- The project sponsor (the CEO) dedicated around 40% of his time to drive the project
- The most talented people were recruited to the team and dedicated 100% of their time to the project

WHAT, HOW & WHEN: HARD AND SOFT ASPECTS OF THE PROJECT
- There was a fixed deadline: 29 June 2007 (the launch was planned for the annual Macworld trade show)
- The project worked with two prototypes (respectively with the iPod and the Mac as their starting points)
- There was an obsession with the quality of the end product

WHERE: ORGANIZATION, CULTURE, CONTEXT AND COMPETENCIES
- Priority number one project that received all the attention and resources needed
- Apple established a project-based organization to design and develop the iPhone

STUDENTS' REAL-LIFE PROJECTS

More and more students are learning through real-life projects. There are several organizations that sponsor and promote this kind of hands-on learning approach, with a tangible impact on society. Better Their World (led by Marc Prensky, founder of the Global Future Education Institute) and the group Design for Change (started in India) are great promotors of this radical new way of educating future generations. Following are just two of the astonishing projects carried out.

IPAD PACT

In 2014, five-year-old students at Rueil-Malmaison, France, were learning how to read and write with the support of senior citizens who came to the school to help out. The students realized that the senior citizens were more afraid of iPads than the children had been of reading and writing. The children had grown up with technology and were used to using it in their everyday lives, but this was not the case for the senior citizens. The tutors and the children brainstormed about the challenges they had observed and developed a project to teach senior citizens how to operate iPads in exchange for their support: to teach the seniors as much as the seniors taught them.

Besides the teaching, to help the seniors feel less lonely, the young children decided to interact and socialize with them by writing postcards and creating posters and gifts for them. They even decided to organize a party to bring the seniors and their families together. Through these actions, the children developed real empathy with the senior citizens. With their childlike mood and ideas, they had a positive impact on the seniors' day-to-day lives. On the other hand, the children built self-confidence and learned how to put ideas into practice. As of this writing, they all keep in touch via Twitter, which is an excellent arrangement for both: the seniors practice using iPads while the children keep practising reading and writing.

This is a good example of a project that, with very few resources but with a clear purpose, has had a real impact in the world, ensuring quality education for its participants and promoting lifelong learning.[124]

ARECIBO OBSERVATORY IN PUERTO RICO

A migrant high school class in Westlaco, Texas, heard from an instructor that the Arecibo radio telescope – one of the largest satellite dishes in the world (approximately 70,000 square metres) – was becoming inaccurate because of the accumulation of algae and debris. During its long history, Arecibo Observatory, Puerto Rico, has served as the home base of large-scale astronomical research projects and has joined the search for extra-terrestrial intelligence.

The experts at the observatory had tried unsuccessfully for over 35 years to devise a way to clean the massive dish. Under the guidance of their instructor, a team of the high school students took up the challenge and started to work on the project. Over the course of a year, the students designed a complex robotic system to clean and maintain the enormous antenna. The manufacturing started in January 2016 in Rio Grande Valley through rapid prototyping.

The project allowed students to learn how to work and resolve an issue through a cross-functional and international project with clear objectives and deadlines. It was also a great opportunity for them to learn how to apply in practice the electronics and programming concepts they had studied in class.[125]

SINGULAR PROJECTS AROUND THE WORLD

SETTING YOUNG PEOPLE ON
THE RIGHT CAREER PATH

Shortly after the global economic crisis in 2008, Europe was hit by a youth unemployment crisis. Certain European countries experienced youth unemployment rates of up to 55%. In the midst of this grave situation, Mr Kamil Mroz and a group of volunteers from Junior Chamber International offered to lead an event-based project to help vulnerable youths in Belgium.[126] The project consisted of inspirational panels with top-level speakers, workshops by career coaches and a face-to-face CV assessment from HR personnel offering feedback to young people trying to get a foot on the job ladder.

After proving to be successful in Belgium, the model was exported to many other countries (including Bulgaria, Latvia, Poland and the UK) as a programme and received numerous national and international accolades. The project was identified as representing best practice by the International Project Management Association. Notable challenges that it overcame included sustaining the engagement of volunteers, building a broad coalition of public and private stakeholders, and adapting a tailored project management approach to a volunteer initiative.

INCLUSIVE DIGITAL EDUCATION FOR CHILDREN WITH SPECIAL EDUCATIONAL NEEDS: 'REDESIGN OUR EDUCATION' IN SMALL WAYS

Mrs Rozina Spinnoy, social entrepreneur, design strategist and mother of three sons decided to launch a project in 2016 to design an education programme. The purpose was to be inclusive of children with special educational needs (SEN) in the digital age. The project goal was to build and nurture the children's skills, with workshops exploring innovative and inclusive processes and to encourage their critical thinking skills, linking creative and digital play. In 2017, the first pilot workshop took place in Brussels, mixing children from an SEN school and a mainstream school. It was incredibly rewarding to be asked by the teachers and one of the schools to help in implementing this programme in their newly renovated school. This incredible project shows us that active citizens, using design thinking, can launch projects that solve some of our societal challenges in small ways that can contribute to systemic change. It shows that it is possible to be more inclusive and to create more sustainable, cohesive societies.

INTRODUCING ELECTRONIC VOTING IN SAN DIEGO[127]

In the early 2000s, a limited number of US states and counties were exploring the possibilities of electronic voting, rather than voting with traditional paper ballots or mechanical voting systems. San Diego County decided to a launch a project to introduce electronic voting, with the support of Mr Ray W. Frohnhoefer. The main purpose of the project was to improve compliance with the legally required and publicly expected timeframes in a county in which the population was steadily increasing. The identification of the countless stakeholders impacted by the project was one of the biggest challenges. Despite the public being sceptical, the novelty and the technical challenges, the project was a success. The benefit of reporting within the legal timeframe was achieved. Thanks to this pioneer project, today, electronic voting is a widespread practice in many US counties.

FOSTERING ENTREPRENEURSHIP
IN AGUASCALIENTES, MEXICO[128]

In December 2016, the Secretary of Economic Development of Aguascalientes, Mexico, launched a project, led by Mrs Eneida Góngora Sánchez, to increase the support given to young entrepreneurs and increase the establishment of successful small and medium sized businesses. Through a public–private partnership with MIT's Enterprise Forum, the team developed a strategic annual programme to foster the entrepreneurship ecosystem, including MIT's best practices for entrepreneurs. Thanks to applying best practices, the project allowed 100 participants to learn one the most successful entrepreneur training models in the world. The project was a great success, generating great diffusion in the media and positioning Aguascalientes as a hub for entrepreneurs.

SOCIAL PROJECT AT THE CENTEC SCHOOL
OF SANTIAGO DE CALI, COLOMBIA[129]

Providing the means to have a decent life to disadvantaged young people with minimal opportunities is a major challenge in many parts of the world. These young people may have little discipline and few rules in life. In 2016, Mr Carlos Uriel Ramirez Murillo launched a personal project to change this. The first phase consisted of showing how, through project management, young people could visualize their lives in a different way, remove the mentality of poverty from their mind and convince themselves that they are the owners of their lives and their destinies. They learned how to start and end a project with a structured method. One of the boys, Kevin, aged 12 and with drug-addicted parents, founded a gang at age 10. He was in permanent contact with drugs and had zero discipline, but he had an admirable desire to improve his life prospects. After the project, he radically changed and decided to focus on the project of his life. Now he is studying and has become a lecturer, teaching other kids how to have a better life. Karol, a 14-year-old girl coming out of a severe depression, with two suicide attempts, followed the same path, and now she is happily teaching other young kids how to find their own path out of poverty.

PROJECT 66: FROM CHICAGO TO LOS ANGELES

In September 2015, Mr Fabio Luiz Braggio took a motorcycle ride on the historic Route 66 in the US, from Chicago to Los Angeles. As a motorcycle lover, one of his dreams was to do this historic route, which is famous for its scenery. Being a temporary endeavour, a trip fits perfectly into the characteristics of a project. Project 66 demonstrates that project management techniques can and should be applied to any real-life situation, far beyond traditional projects in IT and construction. It shows that the benefits of detailed planning for better results can be achieved for personal projects as well, making dreams a reality.[130]

IMPROVING CHILDREN'S LEARNING EXPERIENCES, INDONESIA

The objective of this project, started in 2014, was to build awareness of a child's unique learning profile and empower each learner's potential using psychological and pedagogical activities. It was carried out with the collaboration of the Faculty of Psychology at the University of Gadjah Mada and independent experts in the domains of psychology, education and project management. The research involved hundreds of psychology testers and more than 5,000 volunteer students. One of the main outcomes of the project was a testing tool (called AJT CogTest), which helps parents and educators understand how their child learns best.[131]

PROJECTS INC.

ORGANIZATIONS IN THE PROJECT-DRIVEN ECONOMY: GOVERNANCE, DESIGN AND BEYOND.

The impact of the Project Revolution is vast and will affect every aspect of our lives. In the area of business it will have (if it has not had already) enormous consequences for the way work is being organized.

This chapter describes the implications of this silent disruption in organizations. It examines how the importance of projects, and project-related work, is affecting corporate governance, organizational designs and the prioritization of work.

CORPORATE GOVERNANCE IN THE NEW PROJECT-BASED AGE[132]

With the rise of projects as a main method of work and long-term value creation, Boards of Directors, and Corporate Governance in general, will need to play a bigger role in the selection, prioritization and oversight of strategic projects. Directors will have to learn the fundamentals of projects, and how they can support the executive team to make them successful. In the following section we look at two cases, one good and one not so good, in which the Board played a critical role in governance aspects in selecting and overseeing projects. At the end I explain the DAFO model for corporate governance in the new project drive world.

DIRECTORS' FAILURE TO DRIVE THE STRATEGIC TRANSFORMATION

Kuoni is a Swiss tour operator founded in the early 20th century that was one of the leading packaged holiday providers in Europe in the 1990s. It had become a very successful company, with steady revenues and healthy growth over the past 30 years. It was often cited as an example of travel quality and business accomplishment. However, in 2000 the travel market changed dramatically: thanks to the internet, hotels and airlines were able to create their own websites, and new online travel agents, such as Expedia and TripAdvisor, aggressively entered the market to provide convenient, faster and cheaper services. All of a sudden it was possible for consumers to compare rates and book flights directly. This had a tremendous impact on margins too, especially for older travel agencies such as Kuoni. The firm was severely hit, its operating revenues starting a continual decline lasting several years. Neither the board nor the management fully grasped the profound reasons behind this value erosion. Explanations provided often referred to the impact of idiosyncratic events, such as terror attacks in Egypt. The board failed to recognize the changed dynamics of the travel industry.

It was only around 2005 that the board understood the severity of the situation and that the changes to the travel market were there to stay. The board members launched a strategic initiative to transform Kuoni into an online operator. They announced that it was the firm's top priority and that online sales should drastically increase. They brought in outside expertise to support the change.

However, the digital transformation project failed terribly.[133] The tough question of what to do with the traditional business was endlessly discussed but never concluded. Revenue and margins continued to decline, leading to the announcement, in November 2015, of the layoff of the company's CEO, Peter Meier, and 350 staff.

BOARD INEFFECTIVENESS IN OVERSEEING STRATEGIC PROJECTS

The root cause here is one that the boards of directors of Kuoni failed to recognize: the lack of effective oversight of projects that are strategic for a company, resulting directly in a lack of appropriate management capabilities for these fundamental projects. This story is not the only example of cases where boards of directors and management have:

- **lacked focus**
- chosen the **wrong strategic projects** to invest in (or paid too much for them)
- not been able to **prioritize** with regard to other key activities
- forgotten to implement a **strong governance model** to oversee the successful implementation of a project until it delivers the value promised.

But this company board is not alone: Deutsche Börse's failed takeover of the London Stock Exchange in 2006, the difficulties that Daimler had integrating Chrysler (ultimately resold to the FIAT Group in 2014 for a symbolic dollar), and the more recent difficulties faced in the merger of Lafarge and Holcim can be considered to suffer from similar causes.

However, there may well be a bigger reason to pay attention to the issue of board ineffectiveness. As highlighted previously, most companies will increasingly need to rely on the success of their strategic transformation projects as they enter the digital and project-based age, where speed and complexity will challenge corporations and boards to an unprecedented extent.[134] Digitalization will likely generate large transformation initiatives composed of hundreds of projects and consume significant amounts of companies' resources.

It is increasingly recognized that the execution of corporate and business strategies in the turbulent world we are navigating typically involves successfully running business operations while executing a number of strategic projects that will help to sustain current business, while also capturing promising future business. Based on my own research, organizations, on average, dedicate an unprecedented 30% to 40% of their resources (staff, time, budgets) to project-related activities, which the Project Revolution will accelerate. Yet, today, very few boards have sufficient strategic project implementation capabilities to navigate in the current turbulent environment, and would be well advised to turn their attention to the question. Project implementation and governance expertise is hardly regarded as a key skill for directors. Indeed, few directors would talk of having the competence that Lou Gerstner considered critical in his successful turnaround of IBM.[135] This operational capability and know-how in terms of governance and implementation of strategic projects is a must-have for boards in the new age. Nevertheless, there are two sides to this coin: on the one side, good governance of strategic projects will avoid serious value destruction, while on the other side good strategic project implementation will be essential to navigating effectively in the new project-driven reality. The answer to the question of whether success is related to best governance practices or to exceptional execution capabilities is neither. Successful organizations build and must have both.

There is of course one last justification for having excellent project implementation capabilities, and that is when companies and boards enter crisis, as BP did when it encountered major tragedy with the explosion of the Macondo platform in the Gulf of Mexico in 2010. The initial mishandling of the BP CEO was finally called to an end when President Obama called the recently selected chairman to the Oval Office. When the chairman left the meeting, he promised a $20 billion damage recovery fund,[136] BP's board became fully involved and the project to terminate the crisis finally took a turn towards effectiveness.

GOVERNANCE ASPECTS OF STRATEGIC PROJECT FAILURES

It is important to understand the various root causes of the failure of strategic projects and how they relate to elements of corporate governance. Typically, the evidence indicates that boards are failing to provide sufficient project or programme oversight in multiple ways.

Most frequently, the root cause of failure is investing in projects without in-depth environmental scanning or a thorough study of the costs, benefits and risks related to the initiative. This is closely related to the risk management and financial resource planning duties of the board. This was the case in the Fortis story (see chapter two), where the board of directors failed to assess the extent of the risk they were taking with the investment, and decided not to settle the transaction at the time and to gamble instead by delaying the payment for the acquisition of ABN AMRO. We have also seen the flipside in the case of Apple's iPhone (see chapter six), where up to three years were dedicated to the ideation phase before the project was started. The reality tells us that the iPhone is an exception and that most boards launch critical projects without an in-depth analysis.

Another common mistake is **lack of prioritization**. When organizations execute too many strategic projects without clear prioritization from the top, the company will be spread too thinly: teams will fight for resources, initial commitments to contribute to certain projects will not be respected and most projects will fail to meet their initial cost, time and benefits estimates. This is an undeniable failure of the board and is related to its **duty of providing clear strategic direction** to the organization, a lack of which is clearly illustrated in the Kuoni transformation tragedy. Related to this is the inability of the Kuoni board to take time to reflect upon the larger trends affecting the industry and the ways in which the company would be at risk from these changes. To support boards and senior leaders to improve their prioritization process, I have developed an easy-to-apply framework, the Hierarchy of Purpose, which is explained in chapter eight.

Other strategic projects fail due to **poor oversight and support from the board** during the execution phase. There are various ways in which a board can support and oversee a strategic project, but surely the worst is for project oversight to be one of the many routine items on the board's already cluttered agenda. The board can support a project in many ways: challenging the business case to ensure it is in line with the company's strategy, making decisions on important trade-offs, providing additional funding and resources, controlling the project via a series of key milestones, providing access to experts within its network, or even deciding when the situation requires that the project be terminated.

One of the key realizations is that it is often **poor decision making** and **ineffective governance** of a project that are the root causes of project failure. For example, projects are launched too quickly, without sufficient strategic rationales (sometimes to please one of the board members) or with insufficient resources. They may then be poorly steered, and ultimately continued even after the strategic rationale has largely been reduced (this may be caused by strong egos, either of the project sponsor or the project leader, prohibiting project termination).

One of the structural signs of danger is when projects have long delays and big investment costs, but also benefits that can only be realized after the project is completed (with no early benefits, or no benefits at all in the case of partial completion). Large pharmaceutical and mega-infrastructure projects such as the Channel Tunnel (see chapter four) are good examples. The problem with these kinds of projects is that, once costs have been sunk, further costs can be introduced at any time, and, if the project was worth starting, it is worth continuing at any point in time, even taking into account cost increases in the amount of the sunk costs. So, if a project that costs €10 billion is worth initiating (because the expected benefits are in the amount of €20 billion), then half way to completion, with €5 billion in sunk costs, the future costs could grow by a further €10 billion (i.e. to a total of €15 billion). This can be done again (contractors know this), and leads such projects to often come in way late and beyond budget, as was the case with the Channel Tunnel, whose shareholders lost their initial investment. This leads to one of the main dilemmas for boards and senior executives with regard to projects, which is when to stop and when to continue a project that is not going according to plan.[137]

But let's now look at an example of a board that has demonstrated the right project capabilities – those this book has identified as vital for boards to possess as we enter the project-driven world.

THE RENAULT–NISSAN ALLIANCE: ENGAGED BOARDS IMPLEMENTING A STRATEGIC PROJECT VITAL FOR BOTH PARTNERS

Renault and Nissan signed an alliance on 27 March 1999 that made them develop a joint strategy and work together on their common interests. Both boards approached the alliance with due caution. Nissan was facing imminent bankruptcy, and even its banks had decided not to renew its loans. No other Japanese automobile company appeared ready to provide the substantial help needed for its rescue. Renault's board was aware that, in 1993, Renault had failed in a similar strategic project, the merger of its truck division with that of its Swedish counterpart, Volvo. At the last moment, Volvo had walked away from the deal, fearful for its loss of independence.

This time, both Renault and Nissan were focused on what each regarded as a vital project for their survival as major automobile manufacturers. Indeed, the alliance would guarantee each partner reaching the minimal level required to be competitive, and would further deliver alliance synergies that would address some of the weaknesses of each partner (supply and design on the Nissan side, and manufacturing quality and improvement on the Renault side). Because the companies differed too much in terms of culture, they would remain autonomous, the alliance being primarily financial and secondarily one of sharing know-how, including through the sharing of executive talent, mostly by Renault to Nissan.

As a result of the strategic and complex nature of this project, considerable attention was devoted to project governance and implementation. The two companies set up joint structures at three major levels:

- **board of directors**: with open communications between the two chairmen and the alliance's major executive on the Renault side, Carlos Ghosn
- **corporate and business unit levels**: Ghosn invited some of the major executive talent from Renault to join him
- **operational level**: with a number of joint project task forces where Renault executives were asked to fill managerial deficiencies inside Nissan.

During the first two years, there was some friction due to differences in dealing with employees, internal and external processes, customers, suppliers and market partners. Renault had to implement a reduction in weekly working hours (due to a new labour law that reduced the working week to 35 hours), and to do so it worked closely within new labour market and government policies. Nissan, in contrast, was aggressively showcasing in Japan the merits of long working hours and self-denial for the survival of the corporation.

Before these symptoms became a threatening point of divergence between the two automotive partners, their boards took a step towards planning and executing jointly. The two companies decided to form an entity focused on coordination and governance of the alliance and its benefits. In March 2002, an Alliance Strategic Management Board, under the corporate name Renault–Nissan BV, was created in Amsterdam. It operated at the highest levels of the two organizations.

The Alliance Board concept proved to be a major part of the solution in coordinating the project across the two companies. It was not a traditional corporate board, meeting a couple of times a year. Instead, it met once a month, at a minimum, and acted practically as a programme steering committee.[138] This is one of the must-have best practices for project success, as seen in the Project Canvas. This tight oversight and governance allowed the two companies to combine planning and execution while maintaining a large degree of independence. Indeed, the two companies had joint shareholdings and shared a vital project and an alliance, but remained otherwise independent, managing their respective operations through separate executive committees reporting to the two companies' respective boards of directors. Of course, the fact that Carlos Ghosn was CEO of Nissan, Renault and Renault–Nissan BV provided the necessary alignment at the top and did not allow traditional cultural and policy divergences to set in and gradually poison the collaborative spirit between two very different companies.

The Alliance Board was where the mid-range and long-range strategies of the two companies were led and coordinated. This included all long-term planning for joint projects in advanced technologies and product development. Notably, the board made decisions about vehicles, financial policies, changes in geographic market coverage and new product development. The Alliance Board was also given the authority to create joint companies under Renault and Nissan, and to make decisions about new partnerships and large investment projects.

Ample empirical evidence[139] exists and shows that the alliance had a positive effect on both companies' financial performance. Besides the initial $3.3 billion in cost savings, the combined sales reached 5,785,231 units in 2004. This represents 8% growth from 2003. The global market share of the Renault–Nissan alliance (which is a virtual company, obtained by aggregating the sales of both partners) reached 9.6% and number one position in the world in early 2017.

HOW CAN BOARDS EXCEL IN
THE PROJECT-DRIVEN WORLD?

Nowadays, digital transformation is the biggest, if not the major, strategic challenge for most companies. It encompasses a strategic redefinition of the business (all the way to changing the mission, then involving major changes in a business's 'tripod': target segments, product–service offer and business model). The result of this business redefinition will undoubtedly consist of a number of transformational projects. I believe it is time for boards to take up their responsibility, build their project execution capabilities, and support their executive team and their organization to succeed in this major transformation.

The Renault–Nissan example illustrates the critical nature of the board's contribution and the role of directors in the selection and oversight of strategic projects. Conversely, ignorance of the duties and accountability of directors in these matters, as shown in the case of Kuoni, is a weakness in corporate governance that can have devastating consequences for corporations, destroying vast amounts of value and often bringing corporations to the verge of collapse – or actually being at the root of organizational collapse.

In order to meet this challenge and effectively dispense their fiduciary duties, boards and executives should undertake the following structural and cultural changes, which I have termed the **DAFO model for corporate governance in the new project-driven world:**

1. **D**iscipline: Implement a culture of discipline and accountability.
2. **A**lignment: Align the organization's structure with the new changing reality.
3. **F**ocus: Improve the organization's focus and results.
4. **O**versight: Introduce governance to oversee and support the implementation.

DISCIPLINE

Countries, organizations and individuals need discipline to implement their projects; without it, consistent performance becomes very difficult.

Discipline is defined as "training to act in accordance with rules" or "the activity, exercise, or regimen that develops or improves a skill".[140] It requires practice and helps organizations and individuals to quickly react and perform. One of the most disciplined types of organization, the army, would not be able to carry out its defence programmes without discipline.

Discipline should not be seen as something negative that inhibits innovation. Rather, innovation depends on discipline. Organizations should clearly distinguish between time set aside for creativity and time allocated to project implementation. The best-performing organizations and individuals are able to make this distinction and to move from the creative phase to the implementation phase very quickly. If they spend too much time on innovation, they will be too late by the time they decide to implement the project. The challenge for the board and executive team is to find the right balance between discipline and creativity/flexibility.

Discipline for individuals and employees means that, once a project has been approved, it should be meticulously implemented without being questioned again and again. This does not mean that there is no room for discussion, flexibility and changes, especially if the project faces unexpected issues during the design or implementation phase.

One final, and very important, aspect of discipline is that often the benefits of projects are not seen until the medium to long term. Too much pressure on the short term can eventually be harmful.

ALIGNMENT

The alignment and balance of an organization's activities and structure, combined with the extent to which project activities are deemed important, determine the overall success of project performance and implementation.

More often than not, however, management underestimates or completely ignores this fact, driven by a 'silo mentality'. Some heads of department will operate within their own little kingdoms and find cooperating with other parts of the business difficult. In many cases, the key performance indicators of one department could be at odds with those of another.

Strategic projects – those chosen for their importance in achieving strategic goals – are almost always cross-departmental and require full alignment across the organization. This means that a strategic project, such as expanding the business into another country, requires resources and input from a number of different departments. Facility experts find the location, lawyers handle the legal documents, HR experts recruit the people, salespeople develop a commercial plan and so forth.

Due to the size and critical nature of these projects, alignment and cooperation of all these departments is needed if these projects are to succeed.

FOCUS

Most companies and many employees are highly unfocused. The results of a study by psychologists Matthew A. Killingsworth and Daniel T. Gilbert of Harvard University have shown that human beings are, by nature, unfocused.[141]

At any point, an average of 50% of the population is not focused on what they are doing. In addition, 30% to 40% of employees' time in the workplace is spent tending to unplanned interruptions and then reconstituting the mental focus the interruption caused. This was not the case 20 years ago, simply because the tools of interruption were not so plentiful.

Focus imposes order. It requires energy, work and some pain – which people often try to avoid. Top management has difficulty setting and communicating a ranked list of priorities, and most staff members end up deciding on their own where to put their efforts, which will probably be on easy and irrelevant tasks. This lack of focus creates a huge amount of wasted money and resources, an inability to execute the strategy, project failures, and unhappy and uncommitted employees. Successful individuals are highly focused, and the same applies to organizations. While every business is focused when it is starting out, only those that manage to stay focused will succeed and stay in business.

If a company's top management is not focused, this significantly increases the possibility that the rest of the organization will also be unfocused. Lack of focus not only leads to unhappiness but also to errors, wasted time, miscommunication and misunderstanding, diminished productivity and loss of income. But, when top management is extremely focused, this is transmitted to the staff and the increase in performance is huge.

The benefits of becoming focused are massive – and the good news is that all these issues can be overcome. One of the first things that Steve Jobs did when he returned to Apple in 1997 was to cancel about 70% of the products and hundreds of projects in a couple of weeks.[142] He was convinced that Apple was unfocused and that, in order to survive, the company needed to become highly focused. Jobs managed to transform Apple by increasing focus, and any executive can do the same.

OVERSIGHT

One of the major reasons why traditionally functioning organizations have difficulty supporting and following up on strategic projects is the absence of the right governing structure. Although the CEO, together with the executive board, is ultimately responsible for all company initiatives, the reality is that, today, most companies still lack clearly assigned responsibilities for effective company-wide strategy execution – and this is why such initiatives often fail.

Once the strategic planning department has consolidated the strategic plans for the next three to five years, it hands over the execution to various departments. However, as previously noted, departments within functional organizations concentrate only on the portion of the strategy for which they are responsible. For example, marketing will focus almost exclusively on its marketing plan, which in turn will be broken down into different initiatives, programmes and projects.

Today's governing structure therefore needs a role – a department even – to take responsibility for the strategic, cross-departmental projects, as well as form a consolidated overview of the progress of strategy execution, and, most importantly, flag up when the strategy is not being correctly executed. A standard board agenda item should be included to encourage dialogue around projects and how they can create value for the organization. The fact that this capability is particularly required as we enter the digital age only supports and motivates the creation of this understanding and routine.

Having explained how leaders, boards and individuals need to change to increase success in their projects, let's look at how organizations need to adapt to enhance their agility in responding to market opportunities and changes.

BECOMING AN AGILE ORGANIZATION IN ORDER TO THRIVE IN THE PROJECT-DRIVEN WORLD[143]

In his 1962 book *Strategy and Structure*, Alfred Chandler argues that an organization's structure should be driven by its chosen strategy and that, if it isn't, inefficiency results.[144]

Taking this one step further, the degree to which project activities are reflected in the organization's structure determines overall implementation success. When executives underestimate or completely ignore this fact, organizations fail to evolve (or adapt) as quickly as the business and markets do. As a result, organizations disappear and a large proportion of strategic projects fail.

Most Western companies have a functional or hierarchical structure. The theory behind hierarchy aims at efficiency and specialization. This was ideal for running the business efficiently in a stable world. Departments are divided along a value chain influenced by Michael Porter's value chain model.[145] Traditional companies are generally run by a CEO, a CFO, and often a COO and a CIO, followed by the heads of business units and functional departments. Each has their own budget, resources, objectives and priorities. Hierarchical organizations consolidate information and control on a few people at the top of the company, where all the information comes together. The most essential and strategic decisions are taken by the leading group, often slowly and far removed from the market reality.

What today's organizations really need is a strategy to help people make the decisions. Organizations need to be able to react at the level of where things are actually happening, which is typically at the operating level.

In addition, until recently, departmental success was measured using key performance indicators tailored to each unit or function. For example, the finance department's success was measured by whether it was closing the books and producing the financial statements on time, and the HR department's by whether it had managed to keep good people on board (low turnover) or had finished employee appraisals on time.

A few heads of units tend to establish their own territories, and collaboration across different parts of the business is often troublesome. To the point that it is not unusual to have conflicting performance indicators between departments.

On the other hand, and as explained earlier, the most critical projects, the most strategic ones, are of transversal – company wide - nature. They require resources, time, budgets from every single department in the organization. Without the commitment and contribution of everyone, it is most likely that the project will not succeed.

Cross-departmental – or company-wide – projects in a traditional functional organization always face the same difficulties, some of which are linked to the following questions:

- Which department is going to lead the project?
- Who is going to be the project manager?
- Who is the sponsor of the project?
- Who is rewarded if the project is successful?
- Who is the owner of the resources assigned to the project?
- Who is going to pay for the project?

The silo mentality adds to this complexity, with managers often wondering why they should commit resources and a budget to a project that, although important, would not give them any credit if successful. Rather, a management colleague, often a direct competitor, would benefit.

Within the traditional organizational structure, quick project execution is not possible. Managing just one project in such a complex structure is a challenge, so imagine the difficulty of selecting and executing hundreds of projects of varying sizes.

THE CHINESE WAY[146]

Interestingly, faced with a silo mentality, a lack of agility, attachment to the status quo, innovation paralysis and all the downsides of traditional organizations, Chinese companies have frequently managed to successfully reformulate their organizations. Let's look at three successful Chinese organizational models: Xiaomi, Alibaba and Haier.

XIAOMI

Xiaomi is a mobile internet company focused on smart hardware and electronics. It is one of the most valuable Chinese unicorns (a start-up company with a value of over $1 billion) with a market capitalization of $50 billion. It has been included in the *MIT Technology Review*'s list of the 50 'smartest companies', and founder Lei Jun has appeared on the cover of *Wired*, claiming "it's time to copy China".

The company started life in 2010 and has emerged rapidly. It outstripped Apple's smartphone sales in China within four years. Then, Xiaomi introduced new products to the market at breakneck speed, disrupting, or at least surprising, market incumbents virtually every time. By 2018, Xiaomi had successfully introduced over 40 products, ranging from smart rice cookers and air purifiers to robot vacuum cleaners and smart running shoes.

Xiaomi has gained a lot of attention for its unusual marketing strategy, which relies completely on digital technology. It uses online sales channels and social media platforms rather than heavy-asset retail shops and distributors. The result is a low-cost sales channel that meets the demands of target customers. However, the truly innovative aspect of Xiaomi is how **its organizational model is driven by projects**. Its 40-plus products in the market are not organized in strategic business units and have not become part of the organizational hierarchy.

The company has a relatively flat organizational structure – the seven co-founders are only one line of management away from the engineers and sales teams. The latter make up the largest part of their employee base. Moreover, **the co-founders are required to be involved with projects and new product development directly**. They participate in user interaction, such as on Xiaomi's own platform, and keep up to date with products and projects. Each Xiaomi employee – including the founders – has a contractual responsibility to directly deal with a certain quota of customer requests. A sophisticated digital problem distribution system allocates questions to any suitable employee. Customer proximity has not only become a performance assessment criterion for employees but also a driver for customer-driven projects. **Each new product development is treated as a project** that can be achieved by mobilizing resources inside and outside Xiaomi.

Two features stand out:
1. iteration of product development and customer-driven projects
2. leveraging of an ecosystem of external resources to speed up project execution.

First, Xiaomi uses a new product development approach that focuses on getting prototypes out to the market as soon as possible (i.e. with good-enough products) and actively involves users in fine-tuning and updating the technology and design. The result is a product that is largely co-developed by the community, i.e. closer to the market need, and with a more efficient R&D process. Xiaomi also uses the best-qualified suppliers for components and focuses on integration and design rather than production and hardware R&D. The key competence of Xiaomi is a project-driven structure where the business model, marketing, promotion and design are centred on the customer interaction, rather than the manufacturing side. The result is that the company can deliver good-quality products that customers want without the investments in production and R&D that a traditional organizational model would require.

Second, customer-driven projects gain speed in Xiaomi by leveraging external resources. Following its three original designs – smartphone, TV set top box and router – all other Xiaomi products were developed as projects in collaboration with other companies or entrepreneurs. For example, Xiaomi identified a big market need for air purifiers but could not find a suitable producer. So, it suggested to Su Jun, former associate professor of industrial design at North China University of Technology, that he develop an air purifier and Xiaomi invest in the start-up. Within nine months (by December 2014), the product was developed and launched at a killer price of 899 RMB, only one third of the average market price at that time.

ALIBABA

Alibaba Group is the world's largest and most valuable retailer, with operations in over 200 countries. With over 50,000 employees and a market cap of $520 billion (as of early 2018), it is one of the top ten most valuable and biggest companies in the world. The success of Alibaba can be largely attributed to its innovative organizational structure, a business ecosystem that has fostered the rapid growth and transformation of its businesses since the company began life in 1999. A business ecosystem refers to "a new organizational form where the businesses are interdependent through a variety of equity relationships combining product and service offerings into a customer centric offering".[147]

Alibaba's business ecosystems consist of hundreds of companies, ventures and projects across at least 20 different sectors. But the majority of these are independently run operations, neither part of strategic business units nor subject to reporting structures. In fact, many of the players in Alibaba's business ecosystem are still fairly small in size.

Alibaba is widely characterized as a dynamic system of companies, ventures and projects enabled by digital technology. Instead of directing the development of new products and implementing projects from the top down, Alibaba functions as what is known as a 'gravity provider' and network orchestrator.[148] For instance, Alibaba's core is composed of four ecommerce platforms (Alibaba.com, 1688.com, Taobao.com and Tmall.com) that are home to 700 million users. Moreover, the interdependence between the companies, ventures and projects is not just based on finance and equity, although these are prerequisites to be part of the business ecosystem. The interdependence is found in growth strategies, investment approaches and complementarities between offerings, business synergies and resource sharing. **Entrepreneurial projects in this ecosystem are allowed to fail** without severe consequences for the sustainability of the whole ecosystem, or the careers of top management.

Employees in Alibaba's ecosystem are selected and managed according to alignment of values rather than rules. The key values of Alibaba include putting the customer first, teamwork, embracing change, integrity, passion and dedication. The consequence of such a value-driven approach is encouragement of taking risks, a strong organizational culture and competition. Employees are assessed on a quarterly basis and rated in terms of performance and value, which are seen as equally important. There is no HR guidebook but only a set of strong principles that guide the employees to operate in a highly dynamic environment. They can initiate any project they like without regard to their current company or department. In fact, the ecosystem of Alibaba provides a safe marketplace of resources in which project initiators can implement their ideas without the limits of corporate hierarchical boundaries and complex hierarchical and vertical reporting structures.

Alibaba has made considerable efforts in keeping its business ecosystem entrepreneurial. While the majority of Chinese entrepreneurs are grassroots entrepreneurs who start from zero, a significant number of entrepreneurs in Chinese internet businesses have spun out from the large technology companies. Alibaba has been, by far, the most active generator of new CEOs. By the beginning of 2016, over 450 individuals had emerged from Alibaba to start their own ventures. In total over 250 ventures have been established by former Alibaba employees. Many of these new projects are started within the ecosystem of Alibaba, leveraging its rich resources and opportunities. **New project initiatives and implementation stay within the ecosystem and do not suffer from bureaucracy, department silos or managerial limitations.**

HAIER

Haier Group is today the world's leading brand of major household appliances. It was founded in 1984 and has been the number one white goods supplier since 2009, with 10% global market share and over 78,000 employees (in 2016). The World Brand Lab's listing of the world's 500 most influential brands ranked Haier at the top of the global white appliances list. In 2016 Haier reached revenues of over

200 billion RMB and acquired GE's appliance division for $5.4 billion, a feat previously unimaginable considering its humble beginnings three decades ago. Haier is also one of the first Chinese companies to continuously bring new products to the market. Haier has many examples of products that satisfy special needs in China – for instance, washing machines with quick washing cycles and 15-minute non-stop washing. Ideas for new products do not only come from the minds of the engineers and managers. Many of the product ideas come from the front end of the company, such as people who undertake repairs and salespeople. Haier's Crystal washing machine series is the outcome of several series of user observations, surveys and innovations in terms of spin speed and operating noise.

Since 1998, Haier has been experimenting with new organizational forms with the aim of reducing hierarchy and control and increasing autonomy, with self-organizing work units and internal labour markets. But it was not until 2010 that Haier put a unique project organization platform in place throughout the company.

Haier's first step to create a **platform organization** was to fundamentally reorganize the company's structure. First, the company eliminated strategic business units and managerial hierarchies with the purpose of creating zero distance from the users of its products. The company **reorganized into three project units, with specific focus.** The first unit focused on new product development, marketing and production and it is the closest to the user. A second set of project units is organized around corporate support functions, such as HR, accounting and legal. The third unit is the executive team. Interestingly, the third unit is the smallest and positioned at the bottom of the inverted pyramid. Its role has been redefined as a support function for the customer facing, self-organizing project organizations.

Haier now has thousands of work units, more than 100 of which have annual revenues in excess of 100 million RMB. More recently, the platform has evolved further to allow the work units of non-core products to spin off. Since 2014, external investors have been allowed to invest in promising new products, jointly with Haier's investment fund. For instance, a furniture maker invested in one of the ecommerce platforms (Youzhu.com) that a work unit developed relating to house decoration. To date, 41 such spin-offs have received funding, with 16 receiving in excess of 100 million RMB.

Through measures such as decentralization, disintermediation and the elimination of internal communication barriers, Haier has decreased its number of staff by 45% but has created more than 1.6 million job opportunities.

SUCCEEDING IN THE PROJECT REVOLUTION REQUIRES A LEAN, AGILE AND PROJECT-DRIVEN STRUCTURE

Large organizations with strong top-down leadership and fast implementation, Chinese companies are at the same time highly innovative and adaptive to changing markets through swift project implementation. The cases of Xiaomi, Alibaba and Haier illustrate how these Chinese companies organize and expand their businesses by combining lean, agile and design-led approaches with project-driven structures.

Agile: With the arrival of the internet and subsequent digital technology revolution, the pioneers have been quick to adapt, to the surprise of many international enterprises. Not only the digital natives BAT and Xiaomi but also traditional manufacturers such as Sony and Haier have embraced digital technologies and created competitive advantages in the new era. By embracing digital technologies and deeply embedding them in their organizational structure, these companies have been able to adapt to changing market conditions by iterating product development.

Lean: Operating in the complex and dynamic Chinese market, these companies have designed their organization as a system of work, rather than a system of control. The approach focuses on making decisions by experimenting and learning, and empowering the people who are closest to the customer. Key features of lean manufacturing – such as zero waste, continuous quality and process optimization – are found in these novel ways of organizing. Alibaba's value-driven rather than control-driven management and Xiaomi's iterated development and quick upgrading of products are based on the logic of experimentation and quick learning cycles.

Design thinking: The ultimate goal of reaching zero distance to the customer is shared by these Chinese success stories. Besides increasing responsiveness, this also allows the organization to deal with ambiguity and experiment to explore solutions that customers want to buy. In fact, Chinese companies are by necessity design thinkers: given the highly dynamic market, the continuous emergence of new customers, and the limited loyalty and maturity of the average client, Chinese companies have to get as close to the customer as possible. Many of the new product development projects, such as Haier's Crystal washing machines and most of Xiaomi's consumer electronics products, are exclusively customer driven, rather than product or technology driven.

Project-driven structures: The three organizational models of the Chinese companies Xiaomi, Alibaba and Haier represent entrepreneurial business ecosystems built around customers with structures that thrive in the project-driven world. They have common attributes. First, they have no strategic business units as the dominant organizational structure and means of management governance; second, there is entrepreneurial motivation and dedication; and third, they have relatively simple organizational structures. Moreover, risk taking and new project execution are not limited by the burdens of bureaucracy but gain from resources within the organizational framework of the business ecosystem.

ADAPT OR DIE: IT IS TIME TO CHANGE THE ORGANIZATION'S STRUCTURE

Western corporations have been organized in the same way for the past hundred years. Their hierarchical structures have become one of the major hindrances of innovation, growth and successful project implementation. For many, changing the model has become a necessity for survival.

In the meantime, Chinese companies have experimented and led the way to modern ways of running organizations. The examples described provide three models that could liberate Western companies from their obsolescence. Adjusting the structure, shifting power and breaking the traditional management models is the only way forward. Yet, achieving this requires sacrificing the old individual-driven mindsets for the common good of the organization. It also requires courageous and determined leaders.

RETHINKING PROJECTS

THE PROJECT REVOLUTION
IS ALLOWING SOME
FORWARD-THINKING
ORGANIZATIONS TO MAKE
RADICAL INNOVATIONS
IN THEIR ESTABLISHED
BUSINESS MODELS.

SELLING PROJECTS, NOT PRODUCTS

In the beginning, companies sold products. And then they sold services. In recent years, the fashionable suggestion has been that companies sell experiences and solutions, solving the needs and aspirations of customers.

Companies, indeed, do all of these things. But increasingly, what companies sell are experience projects. To understand the difference, think of an athletic shoe company, such as Nike or Adidas. A focus on products means a focus on selling running shoes. A focus on experiences might mean they sell you a membership to a local running club. A focus on solutions might mean they figure out how to help you reach your goal weight. While these approaches clearly offer more value than simply selling you a pair of shoes, they also have limitations. Selling products limits the revenues a company can make from clients: unless it is innovating and continuously updating its product offering, customer attrition tends to be high, and it can be hard to incentivize repurchases. Selling experiences provides intangible benefits that are hard to quantify and measure, and it often requires a focus on meeting the needs of one single customer, preventing any mass production. Selling solutions became popular in the early 2000s when customers didn't know how to solve their problems. But today, in the internet age, people can do their own research virtually and define the solutions for themselves.

A focus on selling projects instead would mean helping people to do something more specific, such as running the Boston Marathon. Nike could provide you with its traditional sports gear, but in addition could include a training programme, a dietary plan, a coach and a monitoring system to help you achieve your dream. The project would have a clear goal (finish the marathon) and a clear start and end date.

And that is just one type of project. More so than products, the possibilities with projects are endless.

Consider the evolution of Philips. Founded in Eindhoven, in the south of the Netherlands, in 1891 by Gerard Philips and his father Frederik, it began by producing carbon-filament lamps. Its success was achieved by a culture of innovation and the speedy introduction of new products. Over more than a century of profitable existence, the range of products offered by the company has mushroomed. Today, Philips produces everything from automated external defibrillators to energy-efficient lighting for entire cities. It even applies its smart-sensor technology to teeth brushing.

This profusion of products means that Philips is cash-rich, yet sales in the past decade stagnated and concerns about the company have been reflected in its stock price. Faced with this changing reality, Philips took a long, hard look at itself. It identified the absence of focus and lack of strategy implementation capabilities as crucial elements that needed to be addressed. In the mid 2010s, with intensifying competition, the Philips board decided to split the organization into three different companies: Consumer Health, Lighting and Healthcare.

It then went on to launch 'Accelerate', a programme aiming to accelerate growth by transforming each new independent company into a focused organization. At the heart of the transforming changes brought about by the Accelerate programme are projects.

Over the years, Philips had become an intricate blurred matrix. Accountabilities and responsibilities were shared between products, segments, countries, regions, functions and headquarters. It set out to simplify this convoluted and archaic organization structure.

To do so, Philips put projects centre stage. Projects were identified as the best management structure to break up silos and encourage teams to work transversally (end-to-end) in the organization.

As part of this, Philips Health Tech was divided into just three divisions. Essential to making this happen was a substantial increase in the work executed through projects. The shift was from selling customers a few products every year to creating an engaged relationship over decades.

FROM PRODUCTS TO PROJECTS AT PHILIPS HEALTH TECH

One of the biggest challenges facing Philips Health Tech is that the life expectancy of its products is becoming shorter and shorter. Soon after launch, products are copied by the competition, which means they must be priced more cheaply. Soon, they become a commodity. This removes any opportunity for long-term, steady high margins.

Philips has experienced this even with its high-end healthcare products. Shifting its emphasis to selling projects rather than products was a strategic response to this problem.

For example, Philips sells high-tech medical devices. In the past it sold them simply as products (and it still does). But now Philips seeks out the projects in which its products will be used. If a new healthcare centre is being considered, Philips will seek to become a partner from the very beginning of the project, including the running and the maintenance of the new centre.

Among the results of this project focus at Philips is a partnership with Westchester Medical Centre Health Network aimed at improving healthcare for millions of patients across New York's Hudson Valley. Through this long-term partnership, Philips provides Westchester with a comprehensive range of clinical and business consulting projects, as well as advanced medical technologies, such as imaging systems, patient monitoring, telehealth and clinical informatics solutions.

In similar long-term partnerships with Philips, hospitals have been able to significantly improve their radiology volumes and cut MRI waiting times in half. These organizations are seeing a 35% reduction in technology spending, while improving clinical quality.[149]

Philips is not alone in using an increased focus on selling projects as a means of disruptive transformation. At Microsoft, the company's entire focus has shifted to Cloud services, most of which are offered as projects. It now has around 10,000 operating projects. Airbnb, the peer-to-peer online marketplace and homestay network, valued in 2017 at $31 billion,[150] announced that it would start selling 'experiences', small tourism projects, as a way to create new revenue streams and address the increased regulatory scrutiny in some of its bigger markets. The biopharmaceutical industry is also seeking to work with governments and other purchasers on focused treatment programmes, rather than simply offering individual drugs.

THE PROJECT REVOLUTION IMPACTS
THE CORE OF BUSINESSES

Clearly, the Project Revolution and the shift to selling experiences or solution projects rather than products or services presents sizeable challenges to corporations and their business models. These are the key ones:

- **Revenue streams:** Revenues will be generated progressively over long periods of time (i.e. for the duration of the project) instead of right after the sale of a product. This will have an impact on the way revenues are recognized, accounting policies and overall company valuation.

- **Pricing model:** New pricing models will need to be developed. It is easier to price a product, for which most of the fixed and variable costs are known, than a project, which is influenced by many external factors.

- **Quality control:** Delivering quality products will not be enough to meet customer expectations. Implementation and post-implementation services will also have to be of the highest possible quality to ensure that clients repeat-buy projects.

- **Branding and marketing:** Traditional marketing has focused on short-term, immediate benefits. Marketing teams will need to promote the long-term benefits of the projects sold by the organization.

- **Sales force:** The buyer of the project will no longer be the procurement department of an organization; sales will be pitched to the leader of the business. Therefore, the sales force and sales skills will have to be upgraded with strategy and project management competencies.

Stop for a moment and consider what your organization is selling. Is it an experience project? Increasingly, the answer is clear and affirmative. If not, beware – your products might soon become part of a project sold by someone else.

PRIORITIZATION: THE HIERARCHY OF PURPOSE[151]

Prioritizing is usually seen as a personal skill. People prioritize when they look at how they will spend their time today, this week, this month or this year. But prioritizing is also a key organizational and leadership capability. Indeed, how and why organizations and individuals prioritize their activities is vital to their success. Yet, surprisingly, this is one of the least understood and most neglected areas of life. Capacity and gut feeling, rather than strategy and facts, often determine how many organizations and individuals launch projects.

'Priority' can be understood in various ways, but in organizational terms prioritization sets the agenda in terms of what really matters, which is reflected in how resources are allocated – especially the scarce resources of time and money.

In my experience, one of the main reasons that many individuals and organizations fail is due to a lack of a clear sense of what is urgent or simply selecting the wrong priorities. Get your priorities wrong and the effects can be calamitous.

Look at two of the classic corporate failures of recent times – first of all, Kodak. It wasn't that the company didn't foresee the rise of digital photography, but it chose to prioritize the wrong things. In the 1990s, Kodak invested billions of dollars into developing technology for taking photographs using mobile phones and other digital devices. But, in a classic case of Clayton Christensen's innovator's dilemma,[152] it held back from developing digital cameras for the mass market because it feared that this would kill its all-important film business. Meanwhile, the Japanese company Canon recognized the strategic priority presented by digital photography and rushed in.

Similarly, Finnish company Nokia developed the technology for smartphones earlier than most of its competitors, yet it decided not to launch projects in this field and prioritized exploiting existing products. If it had chosen different priorities, Nokia could still be one of the leading telecom operators in the world.

If the executive team doesn't prioritize, middle management and employees will do, based on what they think is best for the organization. At first, we may think this a good practice – after all, empowering people to take decisions has been lauded since the mid-20th century, and which organization doesn't apply this thinking? Yet, without having a prioritized set of strategic objectives, the consequences are often disastrous.

To illustrate this, let's look at the following real example. Samantha worked as a teller in a local bank serving customers. She loved her job, and her father had also spent his entire career in the same bank. However, like many other banks, the company was struggling to survive due to the low interest rates, the increase of competition and the burden of cumbersome regulation. The executive team worked for months to identify a new strategy that would help to turn around the company. They identified two strategic priorities that they believed would secure the company's future.

In a series of town hall meetings, the CEO informed staff, Samantha included, that the new strategy of the bank was based on two strategic priorities:

1. improve customer experience: increase satisfaction by 20%
2. increase efficiency: serve 20% more customers per day.

The message was crystal clear: as long as Samantha and her colleagues kept focused and met the two strategic priorities, the company's future and their jobs were assured.

The day after, Samantha was extra-motivated after hearing her CEO saying that it was in her hands to save the company she cared so much about. She kept in mind the two strategic objectives and started to serve customers as efficiently as possible, always with a smile. This worked fine until a customer started to talk about a personal loss and the terrible situation he was going through. He clearly wanted to talk with Samantha, who was initially pleased with the idea as it would significantly increase customer satisfaction. However, after a few seconds she froze. What about the second strategic objective, efficiency? If she spent a few minutes talking with her customer, her client servicing rate would suffer. What was she meant to do? She didn't know which objective was more important, but it was her decision. And the problem was that all the bank tellers were facing the same dilemma every day.

The executive team thought that they had clearly communicated the strategic objectives that would turn the bank around, but in fact they had created an operational dilemma. The bank didn't improve performance, and many employees who loved their jobs and worked hard to implement the new strategy were fired.

A well-communicated sense of priorities helps to align most of the projects in an organization with its strategies. This alignment is often championed by business thinkers. But the reality of an organization is much more complex than many suggest. Sometimes the strategic objectives are not clear, or nonexistent. Often, there is a gap and lack of alignment between the corporate strategic objectives and the ones from the different business units, departments or functions.

For an organization to prioritize effectively, it has to recognize and articulate what really matters most. In my own career, I have tried to apply the theories and tools available in the market, yet none proved to be successful. They miss pragmatism and require inputs that would take months to collect and would need a large team to keep up to date.

To address the challenges relating to prioritization that I have been confronted with over my career as an executive in several multinationals, I developed a simple framework that I call the **Hierarchy of Purpose.** Boards of directors, executive teams and individuals can all use the tool to rank priorities and select their most important projects.

The Hierarchy of Purpose is based around five aspects: purpose, priorities, projects, people and performance. Each aspect should be considered in turn, and only once an aspect has been pinned down and fully understood should the organization move on to the next.

PURPOSE

Vision and mission have been very popular concepts, yet they tend to be made up of fancy words, often developed by consultants. The terms are often mixed up and their differences are not understood. Therefore, they are hardly ever used when strategic objectives are set, and as a result staff don't know what really matters. Use purpose instead. State the purpose of your organization and the strategic vision supporting this purpose. The purpose has to be sharp and clearly understood by anyone working for your organization. Amazon's purpose –

"to be earth's most customer-centric company"[153] – is compelling enough to avoid any ambiguity within the organization.

PRIORITIES

The number of priorities admitted by an organization is revealing. If the risk appetite of the executive team is low, they will tend to have a large number of priorities; they won't want to take the risk of not having the latest technology, missing a market opportunity and so forth. On the other hand, if the executives are risk takers, they tend to have a laser-like focus on a small number of priorities. They know what matters today and tomorrow. Define the priorities that matter most to your organization now and in the future. Take the example of Amazon (see above): its purpose clearly puts the customer in the centre. Everyone working at Amazon will know when they have to make decisions that the ones related to customers will always come first.

PROJECTS

Strategic initiatives and projects, when successfully executed, bring the organization closer to its purpose and its strategic vision. Nowadays, companies have a large number of projects running in parallel, mostly because it is easier to start projects than to finish them. Very often capacity, and not strategy, determines the launch of projects. If people are available, the project is launched. If not, it is just dismissed. But which projects should organizations really invest in and focus on? And who wants to risk missing a big opportunity? By using the Purpose and Priorities, senior executives are able to identify which are the best strategic initiatives and projects to invest in. This can also help to identify projects that should be stopped or scrapped. Although theorists suggest developing formulas that automate the process of prioritizing and selecting ideas, my recommendation is not to use such a systematic approach. The exercise is mainly to provide management with different orientations and viewpoints, and ultimately the decision has to be made by management based on human intelligence.

PEOPLE

Prioritizing at an organizational level is incredibly difficult. Large organizations are made up of individuals with their own strong sense of what matters. Every individual in an organization has their own list of priorities. These are by their nature self-serving, informed as much by personal ambition and aspiration as by any sense of alignment with the organization's strategy. Yet, as shown in the example of Samantha, employees are the ones who implement the company's strategies. They perform the day-to-day business activities and deliver the projects. They also have to make many minor decisions and trade-offs every day. Creating clarity around the priorities and the strategic projects of the organization will ensure that every employee pulls in the same direction. It is important to allocate the best resources to the most strategic projects and liberate them from day-to-day operational tasks: projects are delivered more successfully when they have a fully dedicated team and a strong, committed and proactive sponsor.

PERFORMANCE

Traditionally, performance indicators don't measure priorities and seldom indicate the progress made towards fulfilling a company's strategy. Project metrics tend to measure inputs (scope, cost and time) instead of outputs. Inputs are much easier to track than outputs (such as benefits, impact and goals). Identify indicators are linked to the organization's priorities and to the outcomes expected from the strategic projects. Less is more in this case, so one or two for each area will do the job. It is better if people can remember by heart how performance is measured. The ultimate goal is to have the few outcome performance indicators embedded in people's minds. Finally, management should have the right information to quickly react to market changes and to supervise the pipeline of new priorities.

THE BENEFITS OF THE HIERARCHY OF PURPOSE

Organizations that have a highly developed sense of priorities – the payoff of using the Hierarchy of Purpose – are in a powerful situation and benefit from a significant competitive advantage. Such organizations can experience significant reductions in costs, as low-priority activities that fail to deliver against clearly articulated measures can be stopped and there is the potential to reduce duplication, consolidate activities and decrease budget overruns. Overall, prioritizing increases the success rates of the most strategic projects, raises the alignment and focus of senior management teams around strategic priorities, and, most importantly, leads to an execution mindset and culture.

One of the main hidden benefits I have seen every time I have used the Hierarchy of Purpose for the first time with top management is that the discussion turns into a very interesting strategic dialogue. For example, the CEO might ask the director of sales, "How are we going to meet that international growth target if currently we only invest in existing markets, or compliance takes up to 60% of our project capacity? Is this sustainable in the long term? What would be the consequences of balancing our portfolio and investing more in growth and cost optimization, and less in compliance?"

Think of your organization's purpose and priorities. Are all of your employees working according to those priorities? Are the activities prioritized in the best interests of the organization as a whole? How would your priorities change if there were a sudden economic downturn?

PORTFOLIO MANAGEMENT: HOW TO OVERSEE AND IMPLEMENT ALL OF YOUR PROJECTS

Besides prioritization, one of the biggest challenges organizations are facing today is how to implement their hundreds of projects, programmes and strategic initiatives while performing their day-to-day activities.

The purpose of portfolio management is to enhance the strategic dialogue at the top of the organization, which is then cascaded to the rest of the organization. Once the executive team understands this, portfolio management can be embedded in the organization and its corporate culture.

Over the past ten years, I have held portfolio management executive positions in a large telecom operator, one of the largest banks in Europe and at a leading pharmaceutical company. After implementing a portfolio management framework, all these companies have seen major improvements in several areas:

- cost reduction of about 15% in the area of project management from stopped projects (including reducing duplication, consolidating projects and decreasing budget overruns)
- increased success rates of the most strategic projects
- increased alignment and focus of senior management teams around the strategic priorities and the strategic projects of the organization
- most importantly, an execution mindset and culture.

I have also noticed that plenty of leading organizations apply portfolio management as part of their strategic management cycle. Some of them are well known, such as Amazon, Apple, Ikea, LEGO and Western Union.

There is a popular misconception that all of an organization's projects should be aligned to one or more of its strategic objectives. However, the reality of an organization is much more complex, and it is impossible to match all projects to strategic objectives. I prefer to ensure that at least the most important projects and programmes – let's say the top 20 projects – are fully aligned with the strategic objectives.

Despite the clear benefits listed above, most executives do not have a good understanding of portfolio management. The first thing that comes to their minds is financial portfolio management – how to deal with stocks, shares and investments. Very few of them relate the concept of portfolio management to projects and strategic initiatives.

Portfolio management provides a frame to help answer the following questions:

- What are the strategic goals of our organization?
- Given these goals, how are we going to achieve them – through projects or day-to-day activities?
- Which projects should we invest in for the long-term interest of our company?
- What is the best use of our existing and future financial and operational capacities?
- Are there any projects we can stop, suspend or delay if there is a sudden economic downturn?

- Do we have the right resources to lead these projects?
- Is it thetiming right?
- What if the projects fail? Do we have a plan B? And are we learning from failures?
- What are the value and the benefits we are capturing from each project?

The most important aspects of a portfolio management framework are:
- A structured approach for **collecting and analysing** all of the new project ideas. This company-wide process must be applied consistently, which makes the next step – comparing project ideas – much easier. Every proposed idea requires a clear rationale and purpose (the first section of the Project Canvas; see chapter five).

  If the potential project involves a large investment and resource commitment, a business case should be developed, including the financial aspects (costs and benefits) as well as qualitative criteria, such as strategic alignment and assessment of risk factors. The ideas for the most strategic projects, such as acquisitions, will often come directly from the executive team; other, more tactical ideas will most likely come from middle management and staff. The point is that everyone can contribute with project ideas, but they should follow the same process.

  It is important to note that projects are not only about business ideas or research and development. Projects also have to deal with organizational improvements, cost reduction, risk management, regulation (both national and international), asset obsolescence (software, hardware and facilities) and so on.

- A method for **prioritizing and selecting** new project ideas. Ongoing projects must also be prioritized, particularly the first time the prioritization process is implemented. The selection process has to be fair and transparent, and based on agreed criteria. The Hierarchy of Purpose is the ideal framework for facilitating the prioritization process. Some additional criteria for analysing the new ideas are the classic net present value, return on investment, payback period, strategic alignment, risk, complexity and interdependencies.

Portfolio management requires cross-checking and validating that all the strategic objectives have the means (and resources allocated) to be achieved, both in the short and long term, either through day-to-day activities or through projects. One very important selection criteria is ensuring that the company has the right competencies and sufficient available capacity to deliver the strategic project; this is determined by performing a capability check. The exercise is mainly intended to provide management with different scenarios. Despite most theories asserting the possibility of automating prioritization and selection of projects, the ultimate decision has to make by the executives based on human intelligence.

- A **strategic roadmap** that lists the strategic projects to be executed. The company's strategic objectives and goals should be clearly reflected in this roadmap. The list of projects should reflect the outcome of the prioritization exercise so that the most relevant are clearly identified. They will require most of management's attention.

As explained earlier, it is important to keep in mind that a project is a dynamic concept: as it progresses along its life cycle, the initial parameters (costs, benefits, duration and scope), used when deciding whether to launch it, will usually change. These changes may have an impact both on the profitability of the project (either because the costs appear higher than expected or because the benefits appear lower than expected) and on the other projects (because of overall budget and capacity constraints). Therefore, changes to the roadmap can occur, but the top projects should not change frequently.

At least once a year, the executive team should ask for input and sign-off on the strategic roadmap from the board of directors. Afterwards it should be communicated and explained to all the layers in the organization.

- A **governing body** – an investment committee or project review board – decides which ideas and initiatives the organization should invest in, but also decides which projects should be stopped or delayed and oversees the successful execution and thus the creation of value for the company. This committee also defines the company's strategic roadmap. The positioning of the committee within the organization and the members who participate in the committee will determine, to a great extent, the impact and success of the entire project portfolio management framework. It is recommended that the chair of the committee should be the company's CEO. The rest of the members should be the executive team.

The committee should report to the board's risk committee and provide regular updates to the board via the CEO. It is highly recommended that one or two directors should have experience leading large, successful strategic projects. It is important to note that very few companies manage to implement a portfolio management framework across all their departments; they are usually implemented within IT, R&D, supply chain or technical departments. In order to work as intended, the committee should oversee all the strategic projects, breaking silos and ensuring that people work more closely together as one company.

- A **gate funding lifecycle** that allows the executive team to undertake effective portfolio monitoring and control of project funding. This process consists of establishing three to five standard phases for a project's lifecycle – for example, feasibility, initiation, planning, execution and close – at the end of each of which there is a 'gate'. At the end of each phase, project feasibility is evaluated and funding is released, but only for the following phase. If a project is not progressing according to plan, if the priorities of the organization have changed or if the market has evolved, the gate system gives top management an opportunity to adjust or to cancel the project before more resources are wasted.

- A **method for monitoring the execution of the strategic roadmap**, which consists of establishing regular reports to top management and the board on the progress of the strategic projects. These regular reports also help management to quickly react to market changes and to supervise the pipeline of new projects.

- Portfolio management should always be linked to two organi-zation-wide processes: the organization's **budgeting cycle** and **enterprise risk management process**. The most traditional way to look at risk management from a portfolio management perspective is to consolidate the risks of each individual project on a global level. However, if the risk appetite of the senior executive team is very low, they will tend to do as many projects as possible so as not to miss out on opportunities. On the other hand, if the executives are risk takers, they will tend to focus on fewer projects. This idea – doing the *right* projects – is another way of looking at risk management as being linked to portfolio management, and I think it will develop over the coming decades.
- Finally, a **process for capturing the synergies and the benefits** through implementing the benefits-tracking process that is used when integrating a company. During an acquisition, synergies are linked to specific milestones in the integration plans. When a milestone is reached that has synergies attached to it – for example, the closure of some shops – then the benefits can be calculated and compared with the plans. The strategic roadmap has to include these 'synergy-delivering' milestones that are attached to specific returns, even for the point at which the project has been completed. By doing so, management has a way of monitoring the benefits of the portfolio of projects.

To conclude, here is a summary of the most important aspects that should be kept in mind when implementing a portfolio management framework:

- Keep the approach simple and pragmatic.
- Use business and strategic language when presenting to executives.
- Focus on the most important initiatives instead of trying to cover the whole spectrum of projects.
- Keep the management framework at a high level and make it a light process – it should not become heavy or tedious.
- Develop clear instructions to ensure consistency in the application of new processes.
- Involve all key stakeholders (business units, departments and functions) in the process from the very beginning.

- Involve all entities contributing to a project in the definition and estimation of the time and cost.

Amid the irruption of the Project Revolution, every organization in the world will have to implement and include sound portfolio management as part of its strategic processes and competencies.

SKILLS REQUIRED TO BE SUCCESSFUL IN A PROJECT-DRIVEN WORLD

In a world that will have more and more projects, the demand for strong project implementation competencies is increasing by the hour. Just by searching on LinkedIn, it is clear that more and more job descriptions require sound project management skills and experience. In two of my previous companies, one of the major skill gaps identified was people capable of leading projects across the organization. Although several of those skills we learn throughout our lives by intuition and practice, and many could claim to be already project leaders, the reality is that the core has to be learned and trained.

The project leader of the future will be a *chef d'orchestre*, a soccer coach, a truly team player. Someone who is able to gather a diverse group of people, each with their own expertise, and create a high-performing team out of the different individuals. Each participant has to have a clear role, feel that they are contributing to the purpose of the project and be appreciated by the others. I strongly believe that anyone can develop into a successful project leader. However, it requires focus, commitment, determination, personal awareness, eagerness to learn and perseverance during times of failure. Here I have grouped into five categories the main qualities needed to excel in the project-driven world.

ESSENTIAL SKILLS

These skills are the hard technical areas of the Project Canvas, mostly around a solid definition of a project. A good project leader should be able to use the available tools and techniques to determine the rationale and business case of a project. They should be able to work with key contributors and partners in defining the scope (whether for a detailed design, technical solution, product or service). The ability to break down the scope into manageable workloads, identify interdependencies, prioritize the work and translate the work into a comprehensive project plan is one of the most important skills in these categories. Everyone can make a plan, but very few can make a well-defined and precise plan. It requires a good understanding of the details – analytical skills – as well as the overall picture – strategic skills. Risk identification and risk management techniques are also essential. Once the project is under way, the project leader needs to establish reporting mechanisms to monitor the execution of the plan and ensure that sufficient quality checks and tests are being carried out. When delays are foreseen, or changes to the plan, a good project leader should be able to analyse the consequences and provide viable alternatives to the sponsor and steering committee.

HOW TO ACQUIRE THESE COMPETENCIES

My recommendation is to follow a training programme on projects and project implementation. There are also year-long master's courses available. Just beware that their content is focused on the added value, not the pure and traditional technical project management. Ultimately, the goal is to obtain a recognized certification that accredits your knowledge. The most common worldwide is Project Management Professional (PMP) certification, from the Project Management Institute. There are others, such as Prince2 practitioner certification, which is well recognized in the UK and Commonwealth countries. A final option comes from the International Project Management Association, which is not as well-known but is a good complement.

TECHNICAL EXPERTISE

These competencies give the project leader credibility among the team and the project stakeholders. They help the leader to have a minimum understanding of the important technical aspects of the project, and provide the ability to communicate in the language of the technicians. The technical skills of the project leader do not need to be too deep, as this can lead to the tendency to end up deciding on and doing most of the work. A certain level of understanding, enough to challenge the teams, is enough. For example, if the project is to implement a new performance monitoring application, the project leader should take the time to comprehend some of the technical aspects of the software.

HOW TO ACQUIRE THESE COMPETENCIES

My recommendation is to be curious and open minded. The bare minimum when starting a project in an unknown domain is to dedicate some time to reading articles, watching videos and looking at analyst reports. The internet will offer stacks of information. There might be online training on some of the MOOC sites. Meet experts if you have access to them. Learn some of the key words and some of the major challenges faced in the industry. Make a summary of what you find out. Despite having taken the time to learn and understand the technical aspects of the project, never be afraid to admit that you are new to the industry or the topic. Highlight that you are eager to learn and appreciate the patience of the people who are giving you information. Don't forget to explain your added value and what you will bring to the project.

ENVIRONMENT AND/OR BUSINESS ACUMEN

Develop a good understanding of the environment in which the project will be implemented. For example, if the project is about increasing access to education, a good project leader will need to have a good appreciation of the different educational systems – which are the most successful, why, and what are the alternatives that fit best the specific needs that the project wants to address. Similarly, in terms of business projects, the project leader should have a minimum understanding of the business, its purpose, its strategy and goals, its main products or services, its key competitors and its main challenges. Additional knowledge of these functions is an asset. Financial understanding is also a must. Being able to connect the project outcomes and purpose to concrete business challenges and priorities is essential for project buy-in and success. Most of the stakeholders, including senior management, will be more supportive towards the project and the project leader whenever that connection is made. The most important capability in this category is to ensure that, from the early stages, the project has a strong focus on the benefits and the impact. Value creation is one of the most critical and sought-after skills in the project-driven world.

HOW TO ACQUIRE THESE COMPETENCIES

Similarly to the technical competencies, the environmental and business ones are extremely broad. When dealing with projects in the business world, the best way to acquire these skills is through a master's in business administration (MBA). MBA programmes are not cheap and require a significant time commitment, yet they cover most relevant aspects of management in general, and provide a strong general understanding of the key facets of a business. Alternatively, there are master's and even online courses (many for free) on specific topics (innovation, finance, strategy, etc.), which are good complements for a project manager.

LEADERSHIP SKILLS

The increased speed of change, the higher complexity, the overlapping priorities, the conflicting objectives, the culture of searching for a consensus, the multiple generations now working at the same time – all these important elements make the implementation of projects much harder than in the past. Managerial skills were mostly enough then. But today, management skills are not enough; project managers have to evolve towards project leadership. They have to be able to provide direction; communicate progress and changes; evaluate, develop and motivate staff; deal effectively with people without having authority by motivating them (working in a matrix); confront and challenge; engage the project sponsor and senior leadership; understand different cultures and how to leverage from them; manage and persuade multiple stakeholders, sometimes ones who are against the project; build bridges across the organization (which will often be silo driven and scarce in resources); create a high-performing team; and dedicate enough time to develop and coach team members.

In addition, a modern project leader has to be able to make effective decisions, be proactive, have discipline and be results driven. Last but not least, a project leader has to be resilient, which is the ability to bounce back from any difficulties and changes that life throws their way – probably one of the most important leadership skills in projects.

Vice Admiral James Stockdale, a Vietnam War survivor, said about leadership: "Leaders' work is divided into three parts: First, the leader defines the current reality. Then the leader looks at the present but sees a better future. And finally, the leader is the one who, after defining reality and seeing a better future, manages to take the steps and lead the team towards that future."[154]

HOW TO ACQUIRE THESE COMPETENCIES

Leadership skills are the most difficult to teach and to develop. Some of them are a bit easier to learn, such as communication, but most of them require awareness, time, practice and perseverance. There are various models that you can use to get an understanding of the topic.[155] The most important step to start growing in this area is to be aware of your personal characteristics, and your strengths and weaknesses. Accept that you are not great at everything. Select one or two areas you want to develop over the next year. You can work on them alone (self-development), following a specialized course and/or by engaging a personal coach.

ETHICS AND VALUES

Project leaders are expected to have strong ethics and personal values. Leadership is a relationship between people. Therefore, the ability to ethically influence others is a major determination of effective leaders.

Leaders are often in the spotlight and become role models for the team members and the organization. In the project-driven world, there is less room for hiding and mismanagement, as projects and their implementation tend to be very visible and to require quick thinking.

Ethics, motivation to act as a role model and developing a plan of action are key aspects that positively affect leadership and a project's outcome. When ethics and values are made a priority and respected, it will have a positive effect on leadership.

HOW TO ACQUIRE THESE COMPETENCIES

Ethics cannot be acquired – they are part of who we are. However, you can develop a code of ethics that will act as a moral guide for you and for your project. This will also help to guide the project team on ethical matters. To develop a code of ethics for you or the project, look at examples of code of ethics from other people and other companies. Then identify your own values: What are my true beliefs? How would I like others to be treated? How would I like to treat others? Share the outcome with your team and discuss whether they feel comfortable with these values. Once the project's code of ethics has been approved, it should be applied and followed by every member of the project, starting with you. Nowhere is the legendary phrase of 'leading by example' more important than in the area of ethics.

In essence, the project-driven world, where robots and artificial intelligence will do most of the routine and administrative jobs, and a large proportion of the expert jobs, will require a significant shift from hyper-specialization to generalization, from technical expertise to facilitator and from manager to leader.

Yet, unfortunately, most schools and universities do not teach those skills today. In the next section I will share the outcome of a joint study that looked into whether business schools teach project management in their MBAs, with appalling results. However, there is some good news. I strongly believe that anyone can train and develop into a successful project leader.

PROJECT LEADERS WILL BECOME THE CEOs OF THE FUTURE

There is a common belief among the project management profession that the project manager is the 'CEO of the project' – that is, they have to answer to a steering committee (the board of directors) and are responsible for the execution of strategic initiatives (organizational performance). If that's the case, why don't more project managers actually become CEOs?

I believe project leaders are, and will be, some of the best candidates to become future executives and CEOs. To carry out their work they have to bring together all the disparate aspects of theory, reality, processes, finances, politics and human nature, and create benefits and clear outcomes.

Project leaders often manage projects across an entire company (businesses, functions, regions, etc.) and get to see the organization as a whole entity rather than from a siloed point of view of a particular function or unit. They are exposed to decision making, which is one of the driving forces of success. Observing how good decisions are made and understanding the analysis that is undertaken to reach those decisions is valuable when moving into a leadership position. When a person demonstrates success in managing enterprise-level projects and leading resources from a holistic perspective, they are a viable candidate to move up to a C-level position (i.e. top management). For those project leaders interested in moving in that direction, it should be a natural end to years of experience within an industry or group of related industries.

So far, however, CEOs have hardly ever come from project management positions. The 'next CEOs' have tended to come from very limited channels (either from within the company or from outside it).[156] In the business world, most chief executives come from:

- **finance**: if the company requires cost containment and/or cost cutting
- **sales or marketing**: if the company has to increase its top line and focus on business development
- **R&D/IT**: if the company is highly technologically driven
- **operations**: as often the COO is the one running the internal side of the business, so it is a natural move.

The question I pose is: do any of these areas give better experience and exposure for what is needed for a top executive than a project leadership background?

I've heard of only a few examples of project management practitioners who made it to CEO level. The best-known is Alan Mulally (for further details and an interview, see the section on the Boeing 777 in chapter six). Alan is an American engineer, business executive and former president and CEO of the Ford Motor Company. He retired from Ford on 1 July 2014. Ford had been struggling during the late-2000s recession, but it returned to profitability under Alan and was the only major American car manufacturer to avoid the need for a bailout fund provided by the government.

Another great example is Klaus Kleinfield, CEO of Siemens from 2005 to 2007,[157] who established and led the Siemens Management Consulting Group. Klaus personally led projects for a number of global Siemens industry groups. This experience gave him a very broad understanding of Siemens' multiple divisions, but at the same time he proved several times that he was someone who could make things happen (i.e. he was good at execution).

Other examples can be found in the US defence industry. Kent Kresa, formerly chairman and CEO of Northrop Grumman, had a stint as a project manager of some of the major programmes his firm was running while he was on the way up.

In the public sector, it is rather different. The top positions are most of the time assigned to party leaders, who often tend to be public functionaries. Although a large part of their duties is policy implementation – which primarily consists of projects – they hardly ever have a strong background in project management. There are some exceptions, nevertheless, that tell us that countries whose leader has implementation experience tend to have higher levels of performance and better standards of living. One of the best recent examples is Mauricio Macri, president of Argentina, who is a civil engineer by education and has extensive experience in the private sector running large projects. His practical approach has set this crisis-prone Latin American country on a positive path. The president of Rwanda, Paul Kagame, embodies another great combination of visionary and 'doer' skills.

Yet, these few extraordinary individuals are an exception to the trend of leaders tending not to come from a project background. However, I have highlighted them as their stories give us some of the answers we will need later when we consider how project leaders can increase their chances of becoming top executives and leaders.

WHAT ARE THE SKILLS AND COMPETENCIES THAT
MAKE AN OUTSTANDING TOP EXECUTIVE?

Becoming a top executive is the greatest leap that an executive can make in their career. What makes it such an extraordinary transition, of course, is the complexity of the role and the skills that are required to manage that complexity successfully. So, what exactly do presidents and CEOs have that ordinary employees don't?

Successful CEOs have the ability to deliver business results by maximizing shareholders' value, measured in terms of EVA (economic value added) or other metrics (such as earnings per share, profits or sales). They must also deliver on any other strategic goals that are defined when they are hired. Being popular and charismatic may help substantially, because emotional intelligence facilitates leadership.

We can learn a great deal about personal development and career progression from a 2015 study that found that more than 70 past and present CEOs of Fortune 500 companies were McKinsey alumni.[158] In 2011 more than 150 McKinsey alumni were running companies with more than $1 billion in annual sales. A great success story is LEGO, which in 2004 appointed as CEO an ex-McKinsey consultant, Jørgen Vig Knudstorp,[159] who managed to turn this legendary Danish firm around and save it from bankruptcy. In fact, McKinsey consultants are by nature project leaders: their core business is executing projects for their customers, but they are also very well versed in content (technical expertise) and have a strong business and environment acumen (often they have an MBA), which, as stated earlier, makes the perfect mix to become top leaders.

Russell Reynolds, one of the leading executive search companies in the world, analysed the characteristics of nearly 4,000 executives, including over 130 CEOs, and found nine attributes, grouped into three categories, that were key differentiating factors:[160]

- **forward thinking**: the ability to plan for the future
- **intrepid**: the ability to perform effectively in complex and difficult environments
  - calculated risk taking: is comfortable taking calculated but not careless risks
  - biased towards (thoughtful) action: is biased towards execution but not too impulsive

- – optimistic: actively and optimistically pursues new opportunities
- – constructively tough minded: is thick skinned and perseverant but not insensitive
- **team building**: the ability to achieve success through others
  - – efficient reader of people: seeks to understand different perspectives but does not overanalyse
  - – measured emotion: displays intensity and emotion but maintains control
  - – pragmatically inclusive: involves others in decisions but also is an independent decision maker
  - – willingness to trust: is comfortable with a variety of people but is not too trusting.

Looking at Russell Reynolds' research, we can see that a project leader, with the development steps advised earlier, would actually embody all nine of these attributes. Therefore, we can conclude that, in a project-driven world, CEOs and presidents will most likely have, or will need to develop, a strong project implementation experience.

I believe that, despite having very similar competencies, project management skills alone don't make a good CEO. However, project management experience should be a must-have competency for many CEOs.

I recently heard that Procter & Gamble (PG), the leading consumer goods multinational, includes a year of managing a project as part of the career paths of their high-potential staff. This is already a good sign that corporations are starting to move in the right direction.

CAN YOU INCREASE YOUR CHANCES OF BECOMING CEO?

Besides the core skills that a project manager will develop throughout their career, which as we have seen are a very solid basis for a potential CEO, there are some additional skills you should develop in order to make it happen:

- You need to have a **vision** to create something that can generate recurring revenues and growth for an organization.
- You need to be results driven and focus on delivering the benefits and impacts of the project. A common path to becoming

a CEO is through sales, which is also a results-driven environment. Plus, successful sales often require navigating the prospect's political environment to close the deal – this is a useful skill to learn. Those who **bring in revenue** will always be more visible.

- Assume **profit and loss responsibilities** beyond your projects. This can be done by gaining business unit (line) management experience.
- Increase your **organizational intelligence competencies**. In general, the best project managers are often not the most popular people in the company. Although they have diplomatic skills, they don't jeopardize their project's objectives or deadlines just to be nice to people, and they don't spend lots of time on internal politics.
- Don't neglect the **soft skills**, including **charisma**, **political prowess** and **strategic vision**, and continuous education in complementary disciplines, such as psychology, finance, sales and marketing. I always say that the people who have the best combination of skills in terms of their potential to become a successful CEO are those who have completed an MBA and are able to deliver projects successfully.
- Last but not least, develop your **entrepreneurial skills**. The ability to take risks, drive an idea and inspire others is often required to become a successful corporate leader.

In summary, most project managers will have the skills to make it to the top. All that remains is to be confident, keep learning and spend time understanding the business. The biggest hurdle for most project managers is understanding that it's not just about planning and organizational skills; it is necessary to really embrace strategic planning, sales and marketing. To become a CEO, a project manager needs to understand how the business or organization runs[161] – the key value drivers, the history, the products and services, the market and the competition – while also being a visionary, looking around corners and putting their ear to the ground.

HOW EDUCATION AND BUSINESS SCHOOLS CAN
DEVELOP BETTER PROJECT LEADERS[162]

As explained in chapter three, human beings have been carrying out projects since the beginning of our existence. Projects are inherent and an essential part of our lives. We have all been carrying out projects throughout our lives. Yet, surprisingly, very few of us have learned how to carry them out, and those who did have done so mostly out of personal interest and motivation. Despite not having any statistical evidence, we can safely make the claim that, given the current education curriculums, neither schools nor universities nor business schools are teaching us how to define, plan and implement projects successfully.

It is hard to explain why there is this significant flaw in our entire education system. However, there is a change in teaching methods on the horizon. Specifically, this involves a move towards project-based learning, which will have a positive impact in the appreciation and understanding of projects in future generations.

One of the areas I have researched extensively over the past years is executive education, and the master's in business administration (MBA) in particular. The reason for focusing on this field is to prove that, despite business schools' claim that they train and prepare the leaders of the future, they have forgotten to teach them to lead projects successfully. According to *Fortune*,[163] about 40% of Standard & Poor's 500 Index (S&P 500) CEOs have an MBA in any given year. It is, by far, the degree with the most representation among such executives. Between 25% and 30% of S&P 500 CEOs have another type of advanced degree, such as a PhD or law degree.

My interest began when I studied for my MBA at the London Business School and found that it didn't offer a vital project management course. I carried out my first study in 2012, and the results were depressing.[164] Only two of the top 100 MBA programmes, according to the *Financial Times*' 2010 ranking of the world's top business schools, taught project management as a core course. The first business school that required its students to take a course in project management was the UK's Cranfield School of Management, which is ranked 26th in the world. The second and last business school that taught project management as a mandatory course was the University of Iowa's Tippie College of Business, ranked 64th in the world.

In 2017, I carried out a similar study with Bocconi's professor PhD Marco Sampietro.[165] We noticed a slightly positive trend: the number of mandatory project management courses in the top 100 business schools had increased from 2 out of 100 in 2012 to 14 out of the top 200 in 2017.

Project management should be a core skill for an increasing proportion of employees, managers and executives. However, while for many employees the need for project management training is often well understood, for executives we have enough evidence, and extensive experience in executive education, to know that the development of and need for these new competencies are not well understood. There is a general misconception about the role that managers and executives play in project management. Normally, the perspective is that project management can be fully delegated to good employees, while executives and directors play a limited role.

So where do future managers, executives and directors go to learn the skills needed to lead a business? Many of them will do an MBA at one of the top business schools. In fact, business schools are particularly relevant as they are well known for creating the next generation of leaders and for strengthening the competencies of existing ones.

KEY FINDINGS OF THE 2017 STUDY

Full-time MBA: Only 4% of top business schools provide project management as part of their core curriculum

The 197 business schools in the study offered a total of 379 MBA programmes (note that 60% of business schools offered more than one type of MBA).

Of the 379 MBA programmes, 137 (36%) of them included a project management course. This could be a promising percentage. However, the vast majority of project management courses were offered as elective courses and not mandatory as part of the core courses. Elective courses are optional; participants can select a few elective courses from a large list of topics. This situation, therefore, does not guarantee that MBA graduates will acquire project management competencies.

The research highlights the worrying fact that, out of the 137 project management courses provided, only 15 were mandatory. This means that only 4% of the MBA programmes offered by the top 197 business schools offer such essential competencies.

MBA programmes	379
Project management – elective	122
Project management – core	15

Executive MBA: Only 2% of top business schools provide project management as part of their core curriculum

If we look at Executive MBAs (EMBA), which are targeted at participants with longer work experience, often with managerial roles and done on a part-time basis, the presence of project management courses decreases.

Out of 248 EMBAs, only 29 (12%) provided project management courses. Of these, 24 were elective and only five were mandatory (2%).

Executive MBA programmes	248
Project management – elective	24
Project management – core	5

Top 10 business schools: Still very disappointing

If we consider the top 10 business schools in each of the rankings, we come to the alarming conclusion that, of the resulting 13 EMBAs, none offer project management courses in their curriculums.

THE MORE POSITIVE TRENDS

While the diffusion of project management in MBAs and EMBAs is not very high, we have to consider the evolution in recent years. In the research I carried out in 2012, 25% of the business schools had project management courses (both core and electives) in their MBAs while the percentage is now 36%, representing an important increase.

If we consider only the MBAs that provide project management as a core skill, in 2012 only two MBAs offered by top business schools provided project management, while today 15 do.

This is very positive news of course. In only five years, the number of project management courses provided by top business schools has significantly increased. Probably no other subject has experienced such an increase in recent years.

However, the current level of diffusion cannot be considered satisfactory. How is it possible that most of the business schools do not embrace project management, a competency that every MBA graduate will need in their career?

FIVE REASONS WHY BUSINESS SCHOOLS HAVE IGNORED
PROJECTS AND PROJECT MANAGEMENT

A **first interpretation** is that project management is a skill that everyone can acquire 'by doing'. A common mode of thinking is that there is no need for formal education; it is not worth learning project management fundamentals or the tools and techniques of this ancient, yet recently formalized, profession. This would lead to the assumption that organizations are quite successful in implementing their projects. Yet, according to research carried out by the Project Management Institute (PMI) in 2016[166] and as highlighted in chapter four of this book, a distressing trend has been revealed: more money is being wasted on projects. The PMI estimated that, on average, $122 million of every $1 billion spent on projects is wasted due to poor project performance.

A **second interpretation** is that all MBA participants already have project management skills and competencies. Based on personal experience in teaching project management to MBA students at some of the few top business schools that provide it, this was the case in roughly 15% to 20% of cases. The vast majority of the participants I have taught over the past ten years have never learned the techniques needed to lead projects successfully. Most have been exposed to projects over their short careers, and some of them have been intensely exposed to project management environments, yet the way the projects were carried out was far from considered good practice. This tendency is also the case for the students of EMBAs, which is even more surprising. All of them had dealt with projects in their careers, yet very few, around 10%, had received any project management training over the course of their careers.

A **third interpretation** is that many MBA participants, at first, do not consider project management to be a core skill for their career. Based on the qualitative feedback received from participants in the study, this is quite often the case. There are still a few, however, who do not change their minds even after taking the course. What is the source of this misunderstanding? There are probably many reasons, one of which is particularly relevant: too often people think that project management is for project managers while in reality project management is a relevant skill for every person involved in project environments. The origin of this misunderstanding may also derive from the vast project management body of knowledge (books, articles, etc.), which is almost exclusively targeted at project managers – a gap that this book tries to address.

A **fourth interpretation** is that business schools are not fully aware of the role and accountability that managers and executives have in projects. Despite advocating for the need for fast change, business schools are very slow in adapting themselves to new competencies demanded by the marketplace. Discussions with some MBA directors suggest that they too have a tendency to relegate project management to operative roles. It is no coincidence that many project management professors work in the operations departments of universities and business schools. Project management is still too often considered an engineering, IT or technical discipline, which leads to neglect of its managerial components and the strategic role that many projects play in transforming an organization. This interpretation is partially supported[167] by considering the type of project management courses delivered. The vast majority of the courses are simply named 'Project Management', and only a few focus on topics relevant for managers and executives (e.g. 'Strategic Project Management', 'Project Portfolio Management' or 'Project Sponsorship').

A **fifth interpretation** is that business schools lack competencies in project management. While this interpretation may seem pretty improbable, often it is true. In fact, while many topics taught on MBAs fit with formal career paths or roles (MBA faculties include mostly professors of marketing, accounting, finance, HR, etc.), project management is only rarely a career path at many universities and business schools. As evidence, there are only a few project management professors worldwide, and many professors who teach project management are also (or mainly) focused on other topics, since those other topics may further their careers.

HOW CAN THE DIFFUSION OF PROJECT MANAGEMENT IN THE TOP BUSINESS SCHOOLS BE INCREASED?

There are several ways in which the gap could be closed, based on the root of the problem.

On the **business schools** side, deans and MBA programme directors need to understand that project management has become one of the most demanded skills by organizations around the world. Execution has become one of their highest strategic priorities, and it is only through project management that this can be achieved. It is necessary to provide students with a better explanation of what project management is really about.

On the **organizations** side, executives and HR departments have started to acknowledge the need to utilize project management competencies in all aspects of their organizations. Having project managers is not enough. Leading organizations are establishing corporate project management offices, project management training curriculums and career paths for project professionals, and they are requiring successful project experience from their high-potential employees. The evidence is there, and the general view is that this trend will only continue.

On the **knowledge** side, the issue is more difficult to tackle. In fact, not all people involved in spreading project management wisdom and expertise (through courses, consulting, books, papers, case studies, etc.) have the competencies or the status to effectively target managers and executives and to make them aware that project management should be a core competency not only for their employees but for them as well.

On the **student** side, if they want to become true leaders and have a successful career, students should carefully consider which business school they enrol in. They should choose an MBA or EMBA programme that includes in-depth project management courses.

THE PROJECT MANIFESTO

WHAT NEEDS TO HAPPEN TO MAKE THE PROJECT REVOLUTION A REALITY.

We recognize the significant importance of projects for our society and humanity at large, and that there are better ways of implementing projects successfully and helping others to do so. Through this work:

1. We acknowledge that governments implement policies through projects and that countries develop and societies evolve through projects; we believe that ideas are made a reality through projects and that, if one day poverty is eradicated from the earth, it will be through a project.

2. We believe projects are the lingua franca of governments, businesses and personal worlds, from the C-suite right through to an individual managing their career and relationships.

3. We are uncovering a new vast disruption; due to the new reality of accelerated change, more and more aspects of our lives are driven by projects, and more and more aspects in organizations are becoming projects; projects are thus becoming an essential element in everyone's professional and personal journeys.

4. In a world that is becoming increasingly automated and robotized, we see projects as the most human-centric way of working.

5. We believe that organizational agility is achieved through projects, which break through silos, reduce management layers and create high-performing teams.

6. We recognize that start-ups and organizations innovate, grow, transform, create long-term value, and achieve their visions and strategic goals through projects; founders, entrepreneurs and CEOs are the ultimate project leaders.

7. We consider our lives to be a set of projects; studies have become projects, and careers have become series of projects too.

8. Our highest priority is to deliver projects better, to reduce the failure rate, to create more value for individuals and organizations, and to create more sustainable development in our economies and societies at large.

9. We see that projects and project management have received very little attention and have been ignored by leading business thinkers, management publications and business schools; we believe that in the past years this deficiency is being rectified.

10. We recognize project-based education as the best and most enduring learning experience for students and adults.

11. We seek recognition of projects and project implementation capabilities as essential for all management and leadership positions; we aspire for it to become part of the curriculums of every school and undergraduate programme; we aim for it to be taught in every business school and MBA programme.

12. We declare that projects and project management should be recognized as a profession.

NOTES

1. These stories contain a mix of fictional and non-fictional information.

2. "How Berlin's Futuristic Airport Became a $6 Billion Embarrassment" (Bloomberg Businessweek), last modified 23 July 2015, https://www.bloomberg.com/news/features/2015-07-23/how-berlin-s-futuristic-airport-became-a-6-billion-embarrassment.

3. Last modified 22 November 2015, http://www.spiegel.de/international/germany/spiegel-investigation-how-the-new-berlin-airport-project-fell-apart-a-868283.html.

4. *Rwanda Reconciliation Barometer* (Republic of Rwanda, 2015), accessed 6 October 2018, http://www.nurc.gov.rw/index.php?id=70&no_cache=1&tx_drblob_pi1%5BdownloadUid%5D=55.

5. Prime Minster Lee Kuan Yew was in office from 1959 to 1990.

6. *Project Management Job Growth and Talent Gap Report 2017–2027* (Project Management Institute, 2017), accessed 1 October 2018, https://www.pmi.org/-/media/pmi/documents/public/pdf/learning/job-growth-report.pdf?sc_lang_temp=en.

7. Google Books Ngram Viewer is an online search engine that charts the frequencies of any word using a yearly count of found sources printed between 1500 and 2008.
See https://books.google.com/ngrams.

8. "The Number of Americans Working for Themselves could Triple by 2020" (Quartz at Work), last modified 21 February 2018, https://work.qz.com/1211533/the-number-of-americans-working-for-themselves-could-triple-by-2020.

9. "US Senate Unanimously Approves the Program Management Improvement and Accountability Act" (Project Management Institute), last modified 1 December 2016, https://www.pmi.org/about/press-media/press-releases/senate-program-management-act.

10. "APM Receives Its Royal Charter" (Association for Project Management), last modified 6 January 2017, https://www.apm.org.uk/news/apm-receives-its-royal-charter.

11. "Stan Richards's Unique Management Style" (Inc.), accessed 1 October 2018, https://www.inc.com/magazine/201111/stan-richards-unique-management-style.html.

12. https://www.gpm-ipma.de/know_how/studienergebnisse/makrooekonomische_vermessung_der_projekttaetigkeit_in_deutschland.html

13. Atif Ansar, Bent Flyvbjerg, Alexander Budzier and Daniel Lunn, "Does Infrastructure Investment Lead to Economic Growth or Economic Fragility? Evidence from China," *Oxford Review of Economic Policy* 32 (2016).

14. Antonio Nieto-Rodriguez, *The Focused Organization: How Concentrating on a Few Key Initiatives Can Dramatically Improve Strategy Execution* (Abingdon: Routledge, 2016).

15. "Organisational Ambidexterity: Understanding an Ambidextrous Organisation Is One Thing, Making It a Reality Is Another" (London Business School), last modified 1 October 2014, https://www.london.edu/faculty-and-research/lbsr/organisational-ambidexterity.

16. "How to Prevent M&A Failure" (Investment Bank), accessed 1 October 2018, https://investmentbank.com/merger-acquisition-failure-2.

17. Antonio Nieto-Rodriguez, *Boosting Business Performance through Programme and Project Management* (white paper, PricewaterhouseCoopers, 2004).

18. "Fortune Global 500" (CNN Money), accessed 1 October 2018, http://money.cnn.com/magazines/fortune/global500/2007/snapshots/7694.html.

19. "Fortis Wins Shareholder Backing for ABN Takeover" (Reuters), last modified 6 August 2007, https://www.reuters.com/article/us-abnamro-takeover/update-1-fortis-seeks-shareholder-approval-for-abn-buy-idUSL0618878620070806.

20. Antonio Nieto-Rodriguez, *The Focused Organization: How Concentrating on a Few Key Initiatives Can Dramatically Improve Strategy Execution* (Abingdon: Routledge, 2016).

21. See https://www.brightline.org.

22. "Rethinking the Decision Factory" (*Harvard Business Review*), Roger Martin, October 2013, https://hbr.org/2013/10/rethinking-the-decision-factory.

23. Personal communication.

24. "What is Project Management?" (Project Management Institute), accessed 2 October 2018, https://www.pmi.org/about/learn-about-pmi/what-is-project-management.

25. ISO 21500:2012 Guidance on project management.

26. Tim Kasse, *Practical Insight into CMMI* (Norwood, MA: Artech House), 2008).

27. *IPMA Competence Baseline version 3.0* (International Project Management Association, 2006), accessed 4 October 2018, https://www.aipm.com.au/documents/aipm-key-documents/ipma_pm_assessment_competence_baseline.aspx.

28. Nigel Bennett, *Managing Successful Projects with PRINCE2* (Norwich: The Stationery Office, 2017).

29. "Project Management" (Association for Project Management), accessed 4 October 2018, https://www.apm.org.uk/body-of-knowledge/context/governance/project-management.

30. "A Brief History of Project Management" (Project Smart), last modified 2 January 2010, https://www.projectsmart.co.uk/brief-history-of-project-management.php.

31. "Project Management: How Much Is Enough?" (Project Management Institute), last modified February 1999, https://www.pmi.org/learning/library/project-management-much-enough-appropriate-5072.

32. Harold Kerzner, *Project Management: A Systems Approach to Planning, Scheduling, and Controlling* (Hoboken, NJ: Wiley 2009).

33. Mark Kozak-Holland, *The History of Project Management* (Ontario: Multi-Media Publications, 2011).

34. "Megaprojects: The Good, the Bad, and the Better" (McKinsey & Company Capital Projects & Infrastructure), last modified July 2015, https://www.mckinsey.com/industries/capital-projects-and-infrastructure/our-insights/megaprojects-the-good-the-bad-and-the-better.

35. "The Art of Project Leadership: Delivering the World's Largest Projects" (McKinsey & Company Capital Projects & Infrastructure), https://www.mckinsey.com/industries/capital-projects-and-infrastructure/our-insights/the-art-of-project-leadership-delivering-the-worlds-largest-projects.

36. Full research and more details can be found in my book *The Focused Organization: How Concentrating on a Few Key Initiatives Can Dramatically Improve Strategy Execution* (Abingdon: Routledge, 2016).

37. Bank of England – GDP evolution from 1900 to 2010.

38. "$1 Million Wasted Every 20 Seconds by Organizations around the World" (Project Management Institute), last modified 15 February 2018, https://www.pmi.org/about/press-media/press-releases/2018-pulse-of-the-profession-survey.

39. "UK 'Wastes Billions Every Year' on Failed Agile Projects" (IT Pro), last modified 3 May 2017, http://www.itpro.co.uk/strategy/28581/uk-wastes-billions-every-year-on-failed-agile-projects.

40. "Why Your IT Project May Be Riskier Than You Think" (Harvard Business Review), accessed 2 October 2018, https://hbr.org/2011/09/why-your-it-project-may-be-riskier-than-you-think.

41. "The Cost of Bad Project Management" (Gallup), last modified 7 February 2012, https://news.gallup.com/businessjournal/152429/cost-bad-project-management.aspx.

42. "The Cost of Bad Project Management" (Gallup), last modified 7 February 2012, https://news.gallup.com/businessjournal/152429/cost-bad-project-management.aspx.

43. "Delivering Large-Scale IT Projects on Time, on Budget, and on Value" (McKinsey), accessed 2 October 2018, https://www.mckinsey.com/business-functions/digital-mckinsey/our-insights/delivering-large-scale-it-projects-on-time-on-budget-and-on-value.

44. "85% of Big Data Projects Fail, but Your Developers Can Help Yours Succeed" (TechRepublic), last modified 10 November 2017, https://www.techrepublic.com/article/85-of-big-data-projects-fail-but-your-developers-can-help-yours-succeed.

45. "Is Spain Squandering Money on Public Infrastructure Projects? Report says yes" (El Pais), last modified 19 June 2018, https://elpais.com/elpais/2018/06/19/inenglish/1529399004_907742.html.

46. Atif Ansar, Bent Flyvbjerg, Alexander Budzier and Daniel Lunn, "Does Infrastructure Investment Lead to Economic Growth or Economic Fragility? Evidence from China," *Oxford Review of Economic Policy* 32 (2016).

47. "Is the $150bn International Space Station the Most Expensive Scientific Flop in History?" (Express), last modified 25 February 2016, https://www.express.co.uk/news/science/647172/Is-the-150bn-International-Space-Station-the-most-expensive-flop-in-history.

48. "The 40-Year Hangover: How the 1976 Olympics Nearly Broke Montreal" (The Guardian), last modified 6 July 2016, https://www.theguardian.com/cities/2016/jul/06/40-year-hangover-1976-olympic-games-broke-montreal-canada.

49. "Russia Blows $51bn on Sochi Winter Olympics as Costs Spiral" (International Business Times), last modified 10 February 2014, https://www.ibtimes.co.uk/russia-blows-51bn-sochi-winter-olympics-costs-spiral-1435507.

50. "Lessons of Boston's Big Dig" (City Journal), accessed 2 October 2018, https://www.city-journal.org/html/lessons-boston's-big-dig-13049.html.

51. "Vietnam PM Halts $10.6 Billion Steel Plant on Environmental Concern" (Reuters), last modified 16 April 2017, https://www.reuters.com/article/us-hoa-sen-group-environment-idUSKBN17I0HI.

52. "£12bn NHS Computer System Is Scrapped ... and It's All YOUR Money that Labour Poured Down the Drain" (Mail Online), last modified 22 September 2011, http://www.dailymail.co.uk/news/article-2040259/NHS-IT-project-failure-Labours-12bn-scheme-scrapped.html.

53. See https://www.telegraph.co.uk/travel/destinations/europe/france/articles/The-Channel-Tunnel-20-fascinating-facts/.

54. "'We Thought It Was Going to Destroy Us … Herzog and De Meuron's Hamburg Miracle" (The Guardian), last modified 4 November 2016, https://www.theguardian.com/artanddesign/2016/nov/04/hamburg-elbphilhamonie-herzog-de-meuron-a-cathedral-for-our-time.

55. "Air Force Scraps Massive ERP Project after Racking Up $1b in Costs" (Computer World), last modified 14 November 2012, https://www.computerworld.com/article/2493041/it-careers/air-force-scraps-massive-erp-project-after-racking-up--1b-in-costs.html.

56. "Wall Street Journal Calls Merkel's Energiewende 'A Meltdown' Involving 'Astronomical Costs'" (No Tricks Zone), last modified 19 November 2017, http://notrickszone.com/2017/11/19/wall-street-journal-calls-merkels-energiewende-a-meltdown-involving-astronomical-costs/#sthash.mWOTwLbO.dpbs.

57. "Healthcare.gov: Government IT Project Failure at Its Finest" (Huffpost), last modified 18 December 2013, https://www.huffingtonpost.com/phil-simon/healthcaregov-government_b_4125362.html; "Colossal Failed Government Projects and What Happened" (Curiosmatic), last modified 17 May 2017, https://curiousmatic.com/colossal-failed-government-projects.

58. "Melbourne Desalination Plant Costs Tax-Payers an Eye-Watering $649 Million in Annual Operating Charges" (Mail Online), last modified 20 May 2018, http://www.dailymail.co.uk/news/article-5749621/Melbourne-desalination-plant-costs-tax-payers-eye-watering-649-million-year-operate.html.

59. "3 Reasons Why Shell Halted Drilling In the Arctic" (National Geographic), last modified 28 September 2015, https://news.nationalgeographic.com/energy/2015/09/150928-3-reasons-shell-halted-drilling-in-the-arctic/

60. "Two Half-Finished Nuclear Reactors Scrapped as Costs Balloon" (Bloomberg), last modified 31 July 2017, https://www.bloomberg.com/news/articles/2017-07-31/scana-to-cease-construction-of-two-reactors-in-south-carolina.

61. See https://www.kickstarter.com/help/stats?ref=footer.

62. "McKinsey Quarterly Five Fifty: Ultralarge" (McKinsey), accessed 2 October 2018, https://www.mckinsey.com/featured-insights/performance-transformation/five-fifty-ultralarge.

63. "What are 'Porter's 5 Forces'" (Investopedia), accessed 24 October 2018, https://www.investopedia.com/terms/p/porter.asp.

64. "Porter's Value Chain" (IfM), accessed 2 October 2018, https://www.ifm.eng.cam.ac.uk/research/dstools/value-chain-.

65. "BCG Classics Revisited: The Growth Share Matrix" (BCG), last modified 4 June 2014, https://www.bcg.com/publications/2014/growth-share-matrix-bcg-classics-revisited.aspx.

66. "The 7 Ps of marketing" (Business Queensland), last modified 21 June 2014, https://www.business.qld.gov.au/running-business/marketing-sales/marketing-promotion/marketing-basics/seven-ps-marketing

67. "Leader's View – Thinkers50" (Antonio Nieto-Rodriguez), accessed 2 October 2018, http://antonionietorodriguez.com/leaders-view-thinkers50.

68. See Frank P. Saladis, "Bringing the PMBOK® Guide to Life" (Project Management Institute), last modified 2006, https://www.pmi.org/learning/library/bringing-pmbok-guide-life-practical-8009.

69. See http://agilemanifesto.org.

70. Darrell K. Rigby, Jeff Sutherland and Hirakata Takeuchi, "Embracing Agile" (Harvard Business Review), last modified 2016, https://hbr.org/2016/05/embracing-agile.

71. "Concorde Prototypes in Production (1967)" (Aviation Week), last modified 7 May 2015, http://aviationweek.com/quest-speed/concorde-prototypes-production-1967.

72. George T. Doran, "There's a S.M.A.R.T. Way to Write Management's Goals and Objectives," *Management Review* 70 (1981).

73. Jim Collins and Jerry I. Porras, *Built to Last: Successful Habits of Visionary Companies* (New York: HarperBusiness, 1997).

74. Jeroen De Flander, *The Execution Shortcut: Why Some Strategies Take the Hidden Path to Success and Others Never Reach the Finish Line* (The Performance Factory, 2013)

75. Personal communication.

76. Personal communication.

77. "How to Be an Effective Executive Sponsor" (Harvard Business Review), last modified 18 May 2015, https://hbr.org/2015/05/how-to-be-an-effective-executive-sponsor.

78. "Understanding Responsibility Assignment Matrix (RACI Matrix)", last modified 2 October 2018, https://project-management.com/understanding-responsibility-assignment-matrix-raci-matrix/

79. "Top 10 Most Expensive Projects In History of Mankind" (Exploredia), last modified 26 January 2016, https://exploredia.com/top-10-most-expensive-projects-in-history-of-mankind.

80. Brian Merchant, *The One Device: The Secret History of the iPhone* (London: Bantam Press, 2017).

81. ISO 9000, clause 3.2.10, defines QC as "a part of quality management focused on fulfilling quality requirements".

82. ISO 9000, clause 3.2.11, defines QA as "a part of quality management focused on providing confidence that quality requirements will be fulfilled".

83. See https://www.britannica.com/biography/Stanislaw-Ulam, accessed on 24 October 2018

84. "French Railway Operator SNCF Orders Hundreds of New Trains that are Too Big" (The Guardian), last modified 21 May 2014, https://www.theguardian.com/world/2014/may/21/french-railway-operator-sncf-orders-trains-too-big.

85. Personal conversation.

86. "The secret origin story of the iPhone" (The Verge), Brian Merchant, last update 13 Jun 2017, https://www.theverge.com/2017/6/13/15782200/one-device-secret-history-iphone-brian-merchant-book-excerpt

87. Brian Merchant, *The One Device: The Secret History of the iPhone* (London: Bantam Press, 2017).

88. PMBOK® Guide – Sixth Edition (2017), https://www.pmi.org/pmbok-guide-standards/foundational/pmbok.

89. *Pulse of the Profession* (Project Management Institute, 2016), accessed 6 October 2018, https://www.pmi.org/learning/thought-leadership/pulse/pulse-of-the-profession-2016.

90. *Preparing the Introduction of the Euro: A Short Handbook* (European Commission, 2008), accessed 6 October 2018, http://ec.europa.eu/economy_finance/publications/pages/publication12436_en.pdf.

91. "Communication Toolkit" (European Commission), accessed 6 October 2018, https://ec.europa.eu/easme/en/communication-toolkit.

92. "How to Prioritize Your Company's Projects" (Harvard Business Review), last modified 13 December 2016, https://hbr.org/2016/12/how-to-prioritize-your-companys-projects.

93. "Urbanisation and health in China" Peng Gong, Song Liang, Elizabeth J Carlton, Qingwu Jiang, Jianyong Wu, Lei Wang, and Justin V Remais (*The Lancet*, 2012).

94. "Case Study: Iceland's Banking Crisis" (Seven Pillars Institute), Anh Nguyen, last modified 13 June 2017, https://sevenpillarsinstitute.org/case-study-icelands-banking-crisis/.

95. "The 10 Year Recovery, and Lessons from Iceland" (Policy Forum), last modified 15 January 2018, https://www.policyforum.net/10-year-recovery-lessons-iceland.

96. "Welcome to Iceland, where bad bankers go to prison" (The Sydney Morning Herald), Robinson and Valdimarsson, accessed on 28 October 2018, https://www.smh.com.au/business/banking-and-finance/welcome-to-iceland-where-bad-bankers-go-to-prison-20160401-gnvn68.html.

97. "Iceland Pulled off a Miracle Economic Escape" (Business Insider), last modified 29 May 2016, http://uk.businessinsider.com/icelands-economy-miracle-2016-5?r=US&IR=T.

98. "Iceland's programme with the IMF 2008-11", Friðrik Már Baldursson, last accessed in 08 November 2011, https://voxeu.org/article/iceland-s-programme-imf-2008-11.

99. *Rwanda Vision 2020* (Republic of Rwanda Ministry of Finance and Economic Planning, 2000), accessed 2 October 2018, https://repositories.lib.utexas.edu/bitstream/handle/2152/5071/4164.pdf?sequence=1.

100. See http://www.nurc.gov.rw/index.php?id=69.

101. "Background Information on the Justice and Reconcillation Process in Rwanda", United Nations, accessed on 26 October 2018, http://www.un.org/en/preventgenocide/rwanda/about/bgjustice.shtml.

102. *Rwanda Reconciliation Barometer* (Republic of Rwanda, 2015), accessed 6 October 2018, http://www.nurc.gov.rw/index.php?id=70&no_cache=1&tx_drblob_pi1%5BdownloadUid%5D=55.

103. "Corruption Perceptions Index" (Transparency International), accessed 2 October 2018, https://www.transparency.org/research/cpi/cpi_early/0.

104. "An Evaluation of Rwanda Vision 2020's Achievements" (East Africa Research Papers in Economics and Finance), Pereez Nimusima, Nathan Karuhanga, Dative Mukarutesi, EARP-EF No. 2018:17.

105. "Story of Cities #37: How Radical Ideas Turned Curitiba into Brazil's 'Green Capital'" (The Guardian), last modified 6 May 2016, https://www.theguardian.com/cities/2016/may/06/story-of-cities-37-mayor-jaime-lerner-curitiba-brazil-green-capital-global-icon.

106. "The Sustainable Transformation of Curitiba" (Contemporary Urbanism), last modified 6 November 2016, https://theurbanweb.wordpress.com/2016/11/06/sustainable-transformation-of-curitiba.

107. "Jaime Lerner, Mayor of Curitiba" (Jaime Lerner Associated Architects), accessed 2 October 2018, http://jaimelerner.com.br/en/mayor-of-curitiba.

108. "Interview with Jaime Lerner" (Smart Cities Dive), accessed 6 October 2018, https://www.smartcitiesdive.com/ex/sustainablecitiescollective/interview-jaime-lerner/21822.

109. Quoted in "Story of Cities #37: How Radical Ideas Turned Curitiba into Brazil's 'Green Capital'" (The Guardian), last modified 6 May 2016, https://www.theguardian.com/cities/2016/may/06/story-of-cities-37-mayor-jaime-lerner-curitiba-brazil-green-capital-global-icon.

110. "H-Day" (99% Invisible), accessed 2 October 2018, https://99percentinvisible.org/episode/h-day; "Throwback Thursday: Hilarity Ensues as Sweden Starts Driving on the Right Side of the Road" (Wired), accessed 2 October 2018, https://www.wired.com/2014/02/throwback-thursday-sweden.

111. "Dagen H, the day Sweden switched sides of the road, 1967" (Rare Historical Photos), accessed on 28 October 2018, https://rare-historicalphotos.com/dagen-h-sweden-1967/.

112. "Dagen H, the day Sweden switched sides of the road, 1967" (Rare Historical Photos), accessed on 28 October 2018, https://rare-historicalphotos.com/dagen-h-sweden-1967/.

113. "Reflection Paper on the Deepening of the Economic and Monetary Union" (European Commission, 2017), accessed 2 October 2018, https://ec.europa.eu/commission/sites/beta-political/files/reflection-paper-emu_en.pdf.

114. "History of Economic and Monetary Union" (European Parliament), accessed 28 October 2018, http://www.europarl.europa.eu/factsheets/en/sheet/79/history-of-economic-and-monetary-union

115. "The History of the Euro" (European Commission), accessed 10 December 2018, https://ec.europa.eu/info/about-european-commission/euro/history-euro/history-euro_en.

116. "The Glorious History of the Best Plane Boeing has Ever Built" (Business Insider), last modified 18 June 2018, http://uk.businessinsider.com/boeing-777-history-2017-6?r=US&IR=T.

117. "First Boeing 777 Delivery Goes to United Airlines" (Highbeam Research), last modified 15 May 1995, https://web.archive.org/web/20110820160122/http://www.highbeam.com/doc/1G1-16824929.html.

118. "777 Model Summary" (Boeing), accessed 6 October 2018, http://active.boeing.com/commercial/orders/displaystandardreport.cfm?cboCurrentModel=777&optReportType=AllModels&cboAllModel=777&ViewReportF=View+Report.

119. Quoted by "The Making of Boeing 777" (IBS Center for Management Research), accessed 6 October 2018, http://www.icmrindia.org/casestudies/catalogue/Operations/The%20Making%20of%20Boeing%20777.htm.

120. "Did You Know That the First 'iTunes Phone' Presented by Steve Jobs Was Not an iPhone?" (PhoneArena.com), last modified 8 June 2014, https://www.phonearena.com/news/Did-you-know-that-the-first-iTunes-phone-presented-by-Steve-Jobs-was-not-an-iPhone_id56973.

121. "Apple Spent Over $150 Million To Create The Original iPhone" (Business Insider), accessed 27 October 2018, https://www.businessinsider.com/apple-spent-over-150-million-to-create-the-original-iphone-2013-10?IR=T

122. See https://www.statista.com/statistics/276306/global-apple-iphone-sales-since-fiscal-year-2007/

123. "How many iPhones did Apple sell last quarter?", Philip Elmer-DeWitt, accessed 27 October 2018, https://www.ped30.com/2017/04/24/apple-iphone-estimates-q2-2017/

124. "DFC2014 France: The iPad Pact!" (YouTube), accessed 2 October 2018, https://www.youtube.com/watch?v=RxH-RZ2rLII.

125. "Weslaco ISD's Migrant Department Presents The Arecibo Observatory Project" (YouTube), accessed 2 October 2018, https://www.youtube.com/watch?v=s2oofmKUwxc.

126. "JCI in Brussels: Setting Young People on the Right Career Path" (The Bulletin), last modified 7 September 2016, https://www.thebulletin.be/jci-brussels-setting-young-people-right-career-path.

127. Personal conversation Mr Ray W. Frohnhoefer.

128. Personal conversation with Mrs Eneida Góngora Sánchez.

129. Personal conversation with Mr. Carlos Uriel Ramirez Murillo.

130. Fabio Luiz Braggio, *Projeto 66* (Brazil: Giostri, 2017).

131. The information in this section was kindly shared by Dr Mohammad Ichsan (Dipl-Ing, MT, PMP, PMI-SP, MCP) and Mr Abi Jabar. See https://www.crunchbase.com/organization/melintas-cakrawala-indonesia#section-overview for further information.

132. This section is based on the article "How Boards Can Create Lasting Value Through Strategic Project Oversight" (NACD), January/February 2018, written with Ludo Van der Heyden, former dean of INSEAD.

133. "Why Kuoni failed (the digital transformation", Jan Sedlacek, accessed on 28 October 2018, https://jansedlacek.net/kuoni-failed-the-digital-transformation/.

134. For a good exposition of this new reality, see Liri Andersson and Ludo Van der Heyden, *Directing Digitalisation: Guidelines for Boards and Executives* (INSEAD Corporate Governance Initiative, 2017).

135. Louis V. Gerstner Jr, *Who Says Elephants Can't Dance?* (New York: Harper Collins, 2002).

136. "Deepwater Horizon oil spill of 2010" (Encyclopaedia Britannica), Richard Pallardy, accessed on 28 October 2018, https://www.britannica.com/event/Deepwater-Horizon-oil-spill-of-2010.

137. For further details, see Barry M. Staw and Jerry Ross, "Knowing When to Pull the Plug" (Harvard Business Review), last modified March 1987, https://hbr.org/1987/03/knowing-when-to-pull-the-plug.

138. Large, complex projects such as the Renault–Nissan alliance are typically referred to in the project literature as programmes. As mentioned earlier, in this book the word 'project' refers to projects, programmes and strategic initiatives interchangeably.

139. Michel Soto Chalhoub, "A Framework in Strategy and Competition Using Alliances: Application to the Automotive Industry," *International Journal Of Organization Theory And Behavior*, 10 (2007), 151-183.

140. "Discipline" (Dictionary.com), accessed 7 October 2018, https://www.dictionary.com/browse/discipline.

141. See Steve Bradt, "Wandering Mind Not a Happy Mind" (Harvard Gazette), last modified 11 November 2010, https://news.harvard.edu/gazette/story/2010/11/wandering-mind-not-a-happy-mind.

142. *Steve Jobs* (Simon & Schuster), Walter Isaacson, October 2011.

143. This section was written in collaboration with Dr Mark Greeven, Associate Professor of Innovation and Entrepreneurship at Zhejiang University's School of Management.

144. Alfred Chandler, *Strategy and Structure: Chapters in the History of the Industrial Enterprise* (Cambridge, MA: MIT Press, 1962).

145. "Porter's Value Chain" (IfM), accessed 2 October 2018, https://www.ifm.eng.cam.ac.uk/research/dstools/value-chain-.

146. This section draws on insights from a decade-long research program at Zhejiang University (2007–2017) that included interviews with hundreds of local Chinese entrepreneurs and investors, as well as executives in large Chinese firms, focusing on the status and development of dynamic capability by local Chinese firms. Specifically, research on the digital ecosystems of Alibaba, Baidu, Tencent, Xiaomi

and LeEco and a proprietary database on their expansion activities is summarized in Mark J. Greeven and Wei Wei, *Business Ecosystems in China: Alibaba and Competing Baidu, Tencent, Xiaomi, LeEco* (London: Routledge, 2017). Research on pioneering Chinese companies and hidden champions is summarized in Mark J. Greeven, G. S. Yip and Wei Wei, *China's Emerging Innovators: Lessons from Alibaba to Zongmu* (MIT Press, forthcoming). See also Mark Boncheck and Sangeet Paul Coudary, "Three Elements of a Successful Platform Strategy," *Harvard Business Review*, 92 (2013); *The Focused Organization: How Concentrating on a Few Key Initiatives Can Dramatically Improve Strategy Execution* (Abingdon: Routledge, 2016).

147. Mark J. Greeven and Wei Wei, *Business Ecosystems in China: Alibaba and Competing Baidu, Tencent, Xiaomi, LeEco* (London: Routledge, 2017)

148. Mark Boncheck and Sangeet Paul Coudary, "Three Elements of a Successful Platform Strategy," *Harvard Business Review*, 92 (2013).

149. "Philips and Westchester Medical Center Health Network Announce USD 500 Million, Multi-Year Enterprise Partnership to Transform Patient Care" (Philips), last modified 16 June 2015, https://www.philips.com/a-w/about/news/archive/standard/news/press/2015/20150616-Philips-and-Westchester-Medical-Center-Health-Network-announce-USD-500-million-multi-year-enterprise-partnership-to-transform-patient-care.html.

150. See https://www.statista.com/statistics/339845/company-value-and-equity-funding-of-airbnb/.

151. The following section was published on a blog in Harvard Business Review as "How to Prioritize Your Company's Project", 13 December 2016, https://hbr.org/2016/12/how-to-prioritize-your-companys-projects

152. See Clayton Christiensen, *The Innovator's Dilemma: When New Technologies Cause Great Firms to Fail* (Boston, MA: Harvard Business Review Press, 1997).

153. "Earth's Most Customer-Centric Company" (Amazon Jobs), accessed 7 October 2018, https://www.amazon.jobs/en/working/working-amazon.

154. "The Principles of Leadership" (Winter), James Bond Stockdale, 1981.

155. See, for example, "Behavioral Theories of Leadership" (Leadership – Central.com), accessed 2 October 2018, https://www.leadership-central.com/behavioral-theories.html; "The Fundamentals of Level 5 Leadership" (Lesley University), accessed 2 October 2018, https://lesley.edu/article/the-fundamentals-of-level-5-leadership; and "The Five Messages Leaders Must Manage" (*Harvard Business Review*), accessed 2 October 2018, https://hbr.org/2006/05/the-five-messages-leaders-must-manage.

156. The exception is when the company performs in a project-based world – by which I mean that a majority of the revenue and employees spend time on individual projects. In that case, a project manager moving up to become CEO is much more likely.

157. Klaus Kleinfeld established and led the Siemens Management Consulting Group (SMC), an organization formed to develop and oversee a corporate revitalization and business improvement program. Under his leadership, SMC transformed from a small corporate cost centre to a highly profitable and respected consulting business that established cutting-edge practices in benchmarking, project management, business re-engineering and innovation.

158. See "The CEO Generator: McKinsey & Company" (New Corner), last modified 21 October 2015, http://www.new-corner.com/the-ceo-generator-mckinsey-company.

159. "Lego CEO Jørgen Vig Knudstorp on Leading through Survival and Growth" (Harvard Business Review), last modified January 2009, https://hbr.org/2009/01/lego-ceo-jorgen-vig-knudstorp-on-leading-through-survival-and-growth.

160. "Making it to the Top: Nine Attributes that Differentiate CEOs" (Russell Reynolds Associates), accessed 2 October 2018, http://www.russellreynolds.com/content/making-it-top-nine-attributes-differentiate-ceos.

161. It is important to distinguish between running the business and changing the business. Usually the work of project managers is around changing the business. However, the most important side of the business is always the running. It is not until a project manager understands how a company runs and how the projects they manage impact the organization that they start to be recognized as a potential leader. I explore this concept further in my book *The Focused Organization: How Concentrating on a Few Key Initiatives Can Dramatically Improve Strategy Execution* (Abingdon: Routledge, 2016).

162. This section is based on joint research carried out in 2017 with Marco Sampietro, PhD, associate professor of practice at the SDA Bocconi School of Management, and with invaluable support provided by Stefano Cavallazzi and Kannan Swany. See Antonio Neito-Rodriguez and Marco Sampietro, "Why Business Schools Keep Neglecting Project Management Competencies," *PM World Journal* 6 (2017).

163. "The MBA Degree and the Astronomical Rise in CEO Pay" (Fortune), last modified 18 December 2014, http://fortune.com/2014/12/18/mba-ceo-pay-connection.

164. See "Why Top Business Schools don't Teach Project Management to Their MBAs?" (Antonio Nieto-Rodriguez), accessed 2 October 2018, http://antonionietorodriguez.com/why-top-business-schools-dont-teach-project-management-to-their-mbas.

165. Antonio Neito-Rodriguez and Marco Sampietro, "Why Business Schools Keep Neglecting Project Management Competencies," *PM World Journal* 6 (2017).

166. *Pulse of the Profession* (Project Management Institute, 2016), accessed 6 October 2018, https://www.pmi.org/learning/thought-leadership/pulse/pulse-of-the-profession-2016.

167. Partially supported because the syllabuses of the courses are not available online, so this evaluation is based on the course titles.

ABOUT THE AUTHOR

ANTONIO NIETO-RODRIGUEZ

www.antonionietorodriguez.com

Antonio Nieto-Rodriguez is the world's champion in project management and founder of the global movement Brightline. He has transformed a tactical topic such as project management into one of the central issues in CEO's 2030 agenda. He argues that projects are the lingua franca of the business and personal worlds, from the C-suite to managing your career or relationships.

Antonio's research and global impact in modern management have been recognized by Thinkers50 with the prestigious award, 'Ideas into Practice'. He has influenced CEOs of leading organizations, preeminent business media such as *Harvard Business Review* and *The Economist*, top business schools like Instituto de Empresa and Duke CE, and renowned thought leader conclaves such as Thinkers50 and the Peter Drucker Forum. He is a visiting professor at some of the world-leading business schools, including Duke CE, Skolkovo, IE, Solvay, Vlerick, and is a much in demand keynote speaker at events worldwide. He is the bestselling author of *The Focused Organization* and contributor to four other business books.

Antonio is one of the few thought leaders that holds a full-time executive position, currently Director of the Project Management Office at GlaxoSmithKline Vaccines. He is Past Chairman of the Project Management Institute, and previously worked at BNP Paribas, Fortis Bank, ABN AMBRO and PricewaterhouseCoopers.

Born in Madrid, Spain, and educated in Germany, Mexico, Italy and the United States, Antonio is an economist with an MBA from London Business School and INSEAD's International Directors Programme. He is fluent in five languages. He can be reached via email:

antonio.nieto.rodriguez@gmail.com